FEMINISM

Opposing Viewpoints®

Other Books of Related Interest

FEMINISM

Opposing Viewpoints®

Jennifer A. Hurley, *Book Editor*

David L. Bender, *Publisher*
Bruno Leone, *Executive Editor*
Bonnie Szumski, *Editorial Director*
Stuart B. Miller, *Managing Editor*

OPPOSING
VIEWPOINTS®
SERIES

Greenhaven Press, Inc., San Diego, California

Library of Congress Cataloging-in-Publication Data

Feminism : opposing viewpoints / Jennifer A. Hurley, book editor.
    p. cm. — (Opposing viewpoints series)
    Includes bibliographical references (p.) and index.
    ISBN 0-7377-0507-8 (pbk. : alk. paper) —
    ISBN 0-7377-0508-6 (lib. bdg. : alk. paper)
    1. Feminism—United States. 2. Women—United States—So-
cial conditions. I. Hurley, Jennifer A., 1973– . II. Opposing
viewpoints series (Unnumbered)

HQ1421 .F46 2001
305.42'0973—dc21   00-032159
                                                          CIP

Greenhaven Press, Inc., P.O. Box 289009
San Diego, CA 92198-9009

"Congress shall make no law...abridging the freedom of speech, or of the press."

First Amendment to the U.S. Constitution

The basic foundation of our democracy is the First Amendment guarantee of freedom of expression. The Opposing Viewpoints Series is dedicated to the concept of this basic freedom and the idea that it is more important to practice it than to enshrine it.

Contents

"Congress shall make no law...abridging the freedom of speech, or of the press."

First Amendment to the U.S. Constitution

The basic foundation of our democracy is the First Amendment guarantee of freedom of expression. The Opposing Viewpoints Series is dedicated to the concept of this basic freedom and the idea that it is more important to practice it than to enshrine it.

Contents

Why Consider Opposing Viewpoints?

"The only way in which a human being can make some approach to knowing the whole of a subject is by hearing what can be said about it by persons of every variety of opinion and studying all modes in which it can be looked at by every character of mind. No wise man ever acquired his wisdom in any mode but this."

John Stuart Mill

In our media-intensive culture it is not difficult to find differing opinions. Thousands of newspapers and magazines and dozens of radio and television talk shows resound with differing points of view. The difficulty lies in deciding which opinion to agree with and which "experts" seem the most credible. The more inundated we become with differing opinions and claims, the more essential it is to hone critical reading and thinking skills to evaluate these ideas. Opposing Viewpoints books address this problem directly by presenting stimulating debates that can be used to enhance and teach these skills. The varied opinions contained in each book examine many different aspects of a single issue. While examining these conveniently edited opposing views, readers can develop critical thinking skills such as the ability to compare and contrast authors' credibility, facts, argumentation styles, use of persuasive techniques, and other stylistic tools. In short, the Opposing Viewpoints Series is an ideal way to attain the higher-level thinking and reading skills so essential in a culture of diverse and contradictory opinions.

In addition to providing a tool for critical thinking, Opposing Viewpoints books challenge readers to question their own strongly held opinions and assumptions. Most people form their opinions on the basis of upbringing, peer pressure, and personal, cultural, or professional bias. By reading carefully balanced opposing views, readers must directly confront new ideas as well as the opinions of those with whom they disagree. This is not to simplistically argue that everyone who reads opposing views will—or should—change his or her opinion. Instead, the series enhances readers' understanding of their own views by encouraging confrontation with opposing ideas. Careful examination of others' views can lead to the readers' understanding of the logical inconsistencies in their own opinions, perspective on why they hold an opinion, and the consideration of the possibility that their opinion requires further evaluation.

Evaluating Other Opinions

To ensure that this type of examination occurs, Opposing Viewpoints books present all types of opinions. Prominent spokespeople on different sides of each issue as well as well-known professionals from many disciplines challenge the reader. An additional goal of the series is to provide a forum for other, less known, or even unpopular viewpoints. The opinion of an ordinary person who has had to make the decision to cut off life support from a terminally ill relative, for example, may be just as valuable and provide just as much insight as a medical ethicist's professional opinion. The editors have two additional purposes in including these less known views. One, the editors encourage readers to respect others' opinions—even when not enhanced by professional credibility. It is only by reading or listening to and objectively evaluating others' ideas that one can determine whether they are worthy of consideration. Two, the inclusion of such viewpoints encourages the important critical thinking skill of objectively evaluating an author's credentials and bias. This evaluation will illuminate an author's reasons for taking a particular stance on an issue and will aid in readers' evaluation of the author's ideas.

As series editors of the Opposing Viewpoints Series, it is our hope that these books will give readers a deeper understanding of the issues debated and an appreciation of the complexity of even seemingly simple issues when good and honest people disagree. This awareness is particularly important in a democratic society such as ours in which people enter into public debate to determine the common good.

Those with whom one disagrees should not be regarded as enemies but rather as people whose views deserve careful examination and may shed light on one's own.

Thomas Jefferson once said that "difference of opinion leads to inquiry, and inquiry to truth." Jefferson, a broadly educated man, argued that "if a nation expects to be ignorant and free . . . it expects what never was and never will be." As individuals and as a nation, it is imperative that we consider the opinions of others and examine them with skill and discernment. The Opposing Viewpoints Series is intended to help readers achieve this goal.

David L. Bender & Bruno Leone,
Series Editors

Greenhaven Press anthologies primarily consist of previously published material taken from a variety of sources, including periodicals, books, scholarly journals, newspapers, government documents, and position papers from private and public organizations. These original sources are often edited for length and to ensure their accessibility for a young adult audience. The anthology editors also change the original titles of these works in order to clearly present the main thesis of each viewpoint and to explicitly indicate the opinion presented in the viewpoint. These alterations are made in consideration of both the reading and comprehension levels of a young adult audience. Every effort is made to ensure that Greenhaven Press accurately reflects the original intent of the authors included in this anthology.

Introduction

"Feminism embodies the belief in the equality of women."
—*Lyn Cockburn,* Toronto Sun, *March 18, 1999.*

*"Feminism has caused a lot of suffering for a great many
... women."*
—*Anita Blair,* Insight, *November 24, 1997.*

In the early 1960s, a woman looking for a job would open her newspaper to find two lists of employment advertisements: one for men, and another for women. Not surprisingly, the jobs available to men were challenging positions with potential for advancement, while those available to women were typically low-paying and involved mundane clerical tasks. Regardless of their education or abilities, women were systematically excluded from opportunities in the workplace. Those women who did establish careers were often paid less than men—an estimated 51 cents per dollar—for the same work.

Today, as a direct result of the women's liberation movement of the 1960s—which urged the passage of anti-discrimination laws in the workplace and challenged societal beliefs that "a woman's place was in the home"—the barriers that prevented women from seeking careers have been eliminated. Although many feminists maintain that women still do not have full equality in the professional world, most people agree that feminism has dramatically expanded women's job opportunities. Over half of the work force is now composed of women, and many women have attained positions of prestige. Sharon Donovan, director of the Alexis de Tocqueville Institute, reports that as of 1996, women owned an estimated 8 million businesses. In politics, the global average for women legislators rose from 7.4 percent to 11 percent between 1975 and 1995. Furthermore, according to the Women's History Project, "now we see women in literally thousands of occupations which would have been almost unthinkable just one generation ago: dentist, bus driver, veterinarian, airline pilot, and phone installer."

Clearly, the advancement of women within the workplace is among feminism's many accomplishments, successes that include voting rights, economic independence and property rights for women, equal opportunities for education, and a greater awareness of rape and domestic violence. However, not everyone agrees that women's entrance into the workplace has been entirely beneficial to women. Some contend that women are now forced to sacrifice their personal lives—either by choosing not to have families or by severely restricting the time spent with their families—in order to survive within a competitive workplace. As columnist Suzanne Fields explains,

> Feminists' changes have made it easier for my daughter to have broader choices than women had growing up when feminism was in its insurgency. She knows she has work options if she chooses them, options that the 1950s generation of mothers did not have. But she has no illusions about what it means to be a working mother. A pressured and stressful job can't compete in the quality of life categories with cooking for her husband and son.

Furthermore, some contemporary women report that feminism simply doubled their responsibilities. Whereas women of the 1950s were responsible for domestic duties such as cooking, cleaning, and child care, many women today still take on a large proportion of these duties—in addition to a demanding career.

Both feminists and "post-feminists"—those who are critical of the classic tenets and goals of feminism—agree that finding a balance between work and family is a crucial issue for women. However, the two groups propose very different solutions to this problem. According to post-feminists, women should shift their priorities from careers to family. Danielle Crittenden, former president of the Independent Women's Forum and the author of *What Our Mothers Didn't Tell Us: Why Happiness Eludes the Modern Woman*, suggests that women should marry and bear children at an early age, stay home to raise their children, and then pursue careers later in life.

Many post-feminists argue that, although women deserve the right to work and receive equal pay for their work, women are happier and more fulfilled in the home—as reflected by polls reporting that the majority of young mothers under 25 prefer the lifestyle of the 1950s. According to writer Amy C. Goldman, feminists should recognize that traditional gender roles can be beneficial to both men and women. She claims that "a better form of feminism would be not to rebel against 'gender roles,' but instead to assert the value of these roles and to ensure their continuing existence. . . . It is where distinctions between the sexes are properly maintained that men and women complement each other and promote each other's happiness." Goldman and others assert that feminists who criticize traditional gender roles devalue the importance of motherhood.

Most feminists, on the other hand, object to the notion that women should revert to traditional gender roles. In their view, the difficulty women experience in managing work and family responsibilities demonstrates a need for changes within the workplace and the home. Betty Friedan, founder of the National Organization for Women and author of *The Feminine Mystique*, which acted as a catalyst for the women's liberation movement of the 1960s, contends that the two primary challenges facing contemporary feminism are to restructure the workplace to create more flexibility for parents, and to alter the assumption that women should bear more of the child-rearing and domestic responsibilities than men. She writes that "what women and men today need [are] real choices about having children . . . without paying an inordinate price or facing dilemmas in their careers. We need to restructure hours and conditions of work. The technology of work today . . . urge[s] us to flextime, with staggered hours of starting and leaving work, and variable schedules during the work week." In addition to more flexible working hours, Friedan and other feminists claim, a national child care program would enable both single and married mothers to balance the responsibilities of work and family.

The opposing views represented by Crittenden and Friedan are part of a larger conflict between conservative and liberal perspectives on feminism. Conservatives, such as Crittenden, believe that feminism has harmed women and society by de-emphasizing the importance of the traditional family, legalizing abortion, and transforming social norms that discouraged women from engaging in premarital sex. On the other hand, liberals, such as Friedan, defend these developments as important steps in helping women attain status equal to men. In the chapters: What Is the Status of Women in America?, How Has Feminism Affected Society?, Is Feminism Obsolete?, and What Should the Goals of Feminism Be?, *Feminism: Opposing Viewpoints* offers a wide variety of opinions about the legacies and the future of the feminist movement.

CHAPTER 1

What Is the Status of Women in America?

Chapter Preface

According to statistics provided by the National Organization for Women (NOW), each year, 1,400 American women die at the hands of their husbands or boyfriends; an estimated two to four million women are battered—at least 170,000 of whom require hospitalization, emergency room attention, or a doctor's care; and 132,000 women report that they have been the victims of rape or attempted rape. Moreover, asserts NOW, many incidents of rape or assault go unreported; in fact, it is estimated that the number of women raped each year is between two and six times the number who report being raped.

Although most people agree that violence against women is an important societal problem, some contend that the alarming statistics cited by feminist organizations misrepresent the issue. Columnist Mona Charen, for example, points out that women also contribute to the problem of domestic violence: Each year, she writes, an estimated 2.1 million men are the victims of severe domestic violence. Charen states that "researcher Murray Straus, analyzing several studies, concludes that 25 to 30 percent of violent clashes between partners are the result only of attacks by women."

The debate over the seriousness of violence against women is influenced by conflicting ideologies about what causes sexual or domestic violence. Feminists maintain that society promotes violence against women by sending a message—through pornography, other media images, and cultural norms—that it is acceptable for men to subordinate women. Others insist that the roots of violence generally lie within violent individuals themselves, not society as a whole.

Examining the incidence of violence against women is one way that society can determine the current status of women. In the following chapter, authors discuss the scope of violence against women and provide opposing views on whether women are the targets of sexism, workplace discrimination, and destructive media messages.

"Basically, [women] haven't come a long way."

Women Are the Victims of Sexism

Andrea C. Poe

In the viewpoint that follows, freelance writer Andrea C. Poe contends that sexism remains prevalent in American society, as evidenced by the the fact that women still have not gained equality in business, the military, sports, politics, and even the home. Unfortunately, writes Poe, women often perpetuate their own inequality by refusing to challenge traditional gender roles.

As you read, consider the following questions:
1. According to Poe, in what ways are women unequal within the home?
2. What one thing has changed radically since the advent of the women's movement, as stated by Poe?
3. What evidence does the author provide to support her claim that women haven't come a long way?

Reprinted with permission from "You Call This Progress?" by Andrea C. Poe, *Toward Freedom*, March/April 1998.

S exism isn't dead. It's alive and well and living in America. It's found alongside the mahogany paneling of corporate boardrooms. It's firmly entrenched in our military barracks. It roams freely in the lucrative locker rooms of professional sports. It's a silent player on the political stage. And it lurks in living rooms across America.

Contrary to what many may believe, this is not the time for feminists to take a bow and exit stage left. The signs that activist feminism is still needed are all around us.

Take business: While it's true that over the past 20 years some women have found cracks in the glass ceiling, far more have not. In the rare cases when a woman is entrusted with the reins in corporate America, she's thrust before the public eye, a rare and exotic bird.

Take the military: Though trained and ranked like men, women are legally banned from performing the highest and most honorable duties required of a soldier—the right to fight.

Take sports: Think football. What if the multimillionaire players were female? And what if half time was met with a gaggle of nubile young men who pranced before stadiums in short shorts, ankle boots, and tight T-shirts, smiling coyly for the cameras? What message would this send to our sons?

Take politics: This one is easy. When a woman can win the presidency of the United States, we'll know that we've begun to make real gains. Only one woman—Geraldine Ferraro—ever made it to the supporting role of running mate in a major party.

Take living rooms: American home-life may be the biggest challenge of all since equality can't be legislated behind closed doors. Little girls still wake on Christmas morning to find dress-up dolls, makeup kits, and kitchen sets, while their brothers unwrap dinosaurs, race cars, and adventure books.

Women continue to be the primary engineers of the cooking, cleaning, and the running of time-consuming household chores. Men remain the masters of the lawn, repairs, and the barbecue pit.

Women's Own Sexism

Unfortunately, it may be women, more than men, who perpetuate traditional gender roles. It's no longer uncommon to see a dad coaching his daughter's soccer team, propping her on his shoulders at a hockey game, teaching her golf. Yet, it remains extraordinary to see a mom doing these things with either her daughters or sons.

Women's own sexism affects not only their children, but is pervasive throughout the culture. Witness the typical wedding or baby shower. Though it takes both sexes to marry and to become pregnant, these parties are thrown for women by women almost exclusively.

LOOK GUYS...WHY DON'T WE JUST SAY THAT ALL MEN ARE CREATED EQUAL... AND LET THE LITTLE LADIES LOOK OUT FOR THEMSELVES?

And it's women who choose to cast aside their names and adopt their husbands'. Women who keep their own name are eyed suspiciously. When I got married earlier this year and didn't change my last name, it wasn't my husband who was upset. It wasn't even his father, my father, or our male wedding guests. It was the women who were disturbed and confused.

An aunt asked, "Then, what will we call you?" as if my own identity had spontaneously combusted. And it was a friend of mine, a single woman in her late 20's, who blurted out, "Aren't you insulting Scott by keeping your name?" Obviously, nobody asked Scott those questions.

But hyphenation isn't the answer, either. Not only are most hyphenations tongue twisters, they generally do little to further domestic equality. Hyphenation is typically the domain of women. It's in the spirit of faith, respect, and unity that women link their husbands' name to their own. The gesture is noble. But since men tend to feel no such compulsion, the dash has done little to create parity in marriage.

While much has stayed the same since the advent of the women's movement, one thing has changed radically. Today, no shame is attached to women who work—and that's big stuff. I was taunted and teased in the late 60s and early 70s when my mother was the only working mom in the neighborhood. Today, there are more working moms than stay-at-home moms. Although this has more to do with declining economic standards than liberation, we'll take any gain we can get.

We Haven't Come a Long Way

Basically, we *haven't* come a long way, baby. Equal pay for equal work remains elusive. Barbie, with her distorted body image, is a perennial favorite. Female athletes are granted neither the respect nor the financial awards of males. It's still much more likely that your senator, doctor, lawyer, and boss are male. And odds are your pre-school teacher, housekeeper, nurse, and receptionist are female.

Feminist is not a dirty word. The opposition has simply coated it with an ugly patina, one that's effectively sticking at the moment. Even those who, 20 years ago, proudly wore the label that stands for equality, now back-step, side-step, and two-step, doing whatever it takes not to be caught in the glare of what is now considered the dirtiest F word of all.

I write this with considerable sadness. My mother, who was the president of Long Island NOW [National Organization of Women], wrote similar words over 25 years ago. Unfortunately, they remain necessary. Sexism's heart beats on.

I await the day when the Shannon Lucids of our culture don't make headlines because they're female, but because they're Americans. If the past two decades are any indication, I fear I may wait until long after life is discovered on the moon.

| *"It is simply irresponsible to argue that American women, as a gender, are worse off than American men."*

Women Are Not the Victims of Sexism

Christina Hoff Sommers

In the following viewpoint, Christina Hoff Sommers, author of *Who Stole Feminism?*, contests the notion that American women are the victims of sexism. The claim that American schoolgirls suffer from a "girl-poisoning culture," she asserts, is simply the latest invention by feminists who want to prove that society "oppresses" women. However, argues Sommers, no evidence exists that women as a group are worse off than men.

As you read, consider the following questions:
1. What statistics does Sommers provide to show that American boys are doing worse than girls?
2. What evidence does the author offer to support her claim that American women are not worse off than American men?
3. According to the author, how does the feminist establishment shape national discussion and policy?

Reprinted from "The 'Fragile American Girl' Myth," by Christina Hoff Sommers, *American Enterprise*, May/June 1997. Reprinted with permission from *American Enterprise*, a magazine of politics, business, and culture.

D id you know that the United States Congress now categorizes American girls as "a historical under-served population"? In a recent education statute, girls are classified with African Americans, native Americans, the physically handicapped, and other disadvantaged minorities as a group in need of special redress. Programs to help girls who have allegedly been silenced and demoralized in the nation's sexist classrooms are now receiving millions of federal dollars. At the United Nations women's conference in Beijing, the alleged silencing and shortchanging of American schoolgirls was treated as a pressing human rights issue.

A "Girl-Poisoning Culture"

Several popular books have appeared in recent years to build up the notion that ours is a "girl-poisoning culture." That phrase is Dr. Mary Piper's and her book, *Reviving Ophelia: Saving the Selves of Adolescent Girls*, has been at the top of the *New York Times* bestseller list. According to Piper, "Something dramatic happens to girls in early adolescence. Just as planes and ships disappear mysteriously into the Bermuda Triangle, so do the selves of girls go down in droves. They crash and burn."

Where did she get this idea? Where did the United States Congress get the idea that girls are a victim group? How did the "silencing" of American schoolgirls become an international human rights issue?

To answer that, consider some highlights of what might be called the myth of the incredible shrinking girl. The story epitomizes what is wrong with the contemporary women's movement. First, a few facts.

The U.S. Department of Education keeps records of male and female school achievement. They reveal that girls get better grades than boys. Boys are held back more often than girls. Significantly fewer boys than girls go on to college today. Girls are a few points behind in national tests of math and science, but that gap is closing. Meanwhile, boys are *dramatically* behind in reading and writing. We never hear about that gap, which is not shrinking.

Many more boys than girls suffer from learning disabilities. In 1990, three times as many boys as girls were enrolled in special education programs. Of the 1.3 million American children taking Ritalin, the drug for hyperactivity, three-quarters are boys. More boys than girls are involved in crime, alcohol, drugs.

Women Are Not Oppressed

What often gets lost in all of the discussions about the problems women face today in the public sphere is the fact that we've traveled a tremendous political and social distance in just thirty years. What also gets lost is the fact that our problems, compared with those of women a hundred years ago, are relatively minor. Women are not "oppressed" in the United States, and they're no longer (politically at least) even subjugated.

Karen Lehrman, *The Lipstick Proviso: Women, Sex, and Power in the Real World*, 1997.

Mary Piper talks about the "selves" of girls going down in flames. One effect of a crashing self is suicide. *Six times* as many boys as girls commit suicide. In 1992, fully 4,044 young males (ages 15 to 24) killed themselves. Among same-age females there were 649 suicides. To the extent that there is a gender gap among youth, it is boys who turn out to be on the fragile side.

This is not to deny that some girls are in serious trouble, or that we can't do better by girls, educationally and otherwise. What I am saying is, you cannot find any responsible research that shows that girls, as a group, are worse off than boys, or that girls are an underprivileged class. So, where did that idea come from? Therein lies a tale.

The Feminist Obsession with Victimology

The reality is, the contemporary women's movement is obsessed with proving that our system is rigged against women. No matter what record of success you show them, they can always come up with some example of oppression. Never is good news taken as real evidence that things have changed. The women's movement is still fixated on victimology. Where they can't prove discrimination, they invent it.

I, for one, do not believe American women are oppressed.

It is simply irresponsible to argue that American women, as a gender, are worse off than American men.

More women than men now go to college. Women's life expectancy is seven years longer than men's. Many women now find they can choose between working full-time, part-time, flex-time, or staying home for a few years to raise their children. Men's choices are far more constricted. They can work full-time. They can work full-time. Or they can work full-time.

The Power of the Feminist Establishment

The reason we hear nothing about men being victims of society, or boys suffering unduly from educational and psychological deficits, is because the feminist establishment has the power to shape national discussion and determine national policy on gender issues.

Feminist research is advocacy research. When the American Association of University Women released a (badly distorted) survey in 1991 claiming that American girls suffer from a tragic lack of self-esteem, a *New York Times* reporter got AAUW President Sharon Shuster to admit that the organization commissioned the poll in order to get data into circulation that would support its officers' belief that schoolgirls were being short-changed. Usually, of course, belief comes after, not before, data-gathering. But advocacy research doesn't work that way. With advocacy research, first you believe, and then you gather figures you can use to convince people you are right.

The myth of the short-changed schoolgirl is a perfect example of everything that's gone wrong with contemporary feminism. It's all there: the mendacious advocacy research, the mean-spiritedness to men that extends even to little boys, the irresponsible victimology, the outcry against being "oppressed," coupled with massive lobbying for government action.

The truth is, American women are the freest in the world. Anyone who doesn't see this simply lacks common sense.

| *"Generally men still earn more than women, even for the same job."*

Women Face Discrimination in the Workplace

Ida L. Castro

Ida L. Castro contends in the following viewpoint that women do not receive equal treatment in the workplace. She states that women are often paid less than men for the same job, due to women's refusal to respond favorably to sexual advances made by male employers, and the pervasive belief that women's work is somehow worth less than men's—even when that work involves the same skills and responsibilities. Furthermore, Castro writes, traditionally female occupations pay much less than traditionally male occupations. Castro is the director-designate of the Women's Bureau of the U.S. Department of Labor, a federal agency that promotes the welfare of wage-earning women. She is also an attorney who is actively involved in women's and labor issues.

As you read, consider the following questions:
1. What is the wage gap between men's and women's earnings, as cited by Castro?
2. As explained by the author, what factors lead women into traditionally female occupations?
3. What is fair pay or pay equity, as defined by the author?

M ore women than ever are in the labor force—62 million in 1996. A majority of women at all educational levels now work outside the home during the years they are raising children. Yet, we still face some of the underpinnings of the stubborn wage gap between men and women that belong more to the 1950s than to the 1990s.

Women have made dramatic gains in the past few decades, both in education and in the workplace. More women are attending and graduating from college than in the past; equal proportions (almost one-quarter) of young women and men (between the ages of twenty-five and thirty-four) now have college degrees. Women are moving into professions traditionally dominated by men, although job segregation and a gender-earnings gap are still evident.

Women's labor-force participation is still lower than men's. This difference may be attributed in part to the fact that many mothers work part-time, while others drop out of the paid labor force entirely to attend to children. But in recent decades, the economic activity of the two genders has become more similar than different. For adults in their prime working ages (twenty-five to fifty-four), the gender gap in labor-force participation is narrowing. In 1950, the participation rate of men in these ages was 97 percent, 60 percentage points higher than that of women of the same age (37 percent). By 1995, men's participation slipped to 92 percent while women's rate increased dramatically, to 76 percent. Thus, the gap differentiating men and women, although still sizable, has fallen to 16 percentage points.

Beginning in the mid-1970s, more married women have earned wages to provide for their families, and men's wages have declined. The percentage of mothers raising children alone has risen almost 10 points since 1975, making these families slightly more than one-quarter of all families with children in 1996, according to the U.S. Bureau of Labor Statistics. These women have lower incomes and are more likely to be poor than married women, because of women's generally low wages and because of the lack of financial support from their husbands. Women, with or without husbands, deserve a fair wage for their work.

In the past, the common practice of paying men more

than women for the same work was widely accepted because men had families to support. Today, this practice is illegal, but generally men still earn more than women, even for the same job. The disparity has seriously disadvantaged women and their families.

The proportion of women who work while they are married and during most of their mothering years has skyrocketed in the last generation. Now most women have families to support, too, either on their own or along with men. In 1978, for the first time, the majority of mothers were in the labor market rather than at home.

The Wage Gap Between Men and Women

- In 1995, women working full-time and year-round averaged 71 cents for each dollar that men earned.
- African-American women earned only 63 cents and Hispanic women only 57 cents for each dollar earned by white men.
- Women and people of color, on average, earned less than white men with the same educational backgrounds; often, white men with less education earned the same as or more than educated women and people of color. For example, the average college-educated Hispanic woman earned only $21 per week more than white male *high school* graduates.
- Over a woman's lifetime, unequal pay hurts a lot. It directly affects how much—or how little—her pension and Social Security payments will be. Getting old often means becoming poor—for many women and people of color.

Many Women Still Work in "Women's" Jobs

By the end of the 1980s, after two decades of younger women increasing their labor-force participation, women were more often found in higher-paid occupations. In particular, the proportion of managers who were women jumped from approximately one in five in 1970 to close to half (46 percent) by 1996, an increase that paralleled the feminization of business majors in college.

However, women still often end up in traditionally female

occupations, regardless of education. Women and men study different fields in college; women end up as teachers and office workers, men as engineers. In 1996, women held 77 percent of administrative-support positions. Although women's presence increased somewhat, the traditionally male, blue-collar occupations have remained male dominated.

Despite considerable progress, in 1995 women still had not reached earning parity with men. Do women simply choose traditionally female jobs that allow them flexibility and a better chance of being hired? Have the overt barriers of sex-segregated, help-wanted ads given way to less visible barriers against women's full participation in the labor force, often called "the glass ceiling"?

The Wage Gap Widens During Most of Women's Working Years

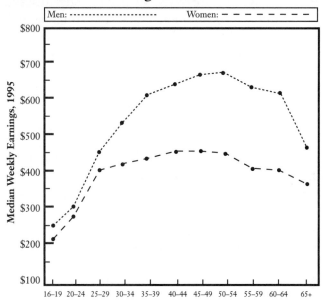

Source: Unpublished tabulations, Bureau of Labor Statistics, Current Population Survey.

Some are of the opinion that the choices women make may contribute to women's lower earnings. Others may argue that women may have invested less in education because they did not expect to work for pay as long as men. Still others believe that women may choose occupations that fit in with assuming primary responsibility for child-rearing, such as temporary or part-time administrative or sales jobs.

As Bianchi and Spain show, working women pay a steep price for flexibility because these jobs pay less, have fewer benefits, and offer little advancement potential. When women leave the labor force to raise children, their skills stagnate, and their reentry wages are low. The value women place on making time for raising children can contribute to occupational segregation, as long as fathers are not committed to spending similar time raising their children.

Other analysts note the continuing influence of "steering" women toward traditionally female occupations. Schools, families, and society at large still remark upon exceptions to the rule that women work in "women's" jobs. Although civil rights laws have for thirty years barred gender discrimination in hiring, pay, promotion, and termination, women applying for nontraditional jobs and women workers throughout the labor force still frequently encounter overt and covert discrimination. As a result, women workers continue to win multimillion-dollar job-discrimination lawsuits, focusing on inequalities in hiring, pay, and promotion.

Getting the Facts About Working Women's Pay

In 1994, the Women's Bureau did both a popular and a scientific sampling of what it means to be a working woman in America today. Its *Working Women Count!* report reflects a consensus among working women about what is wrong with their jobs and what needs to be fixed—a consensus that crosses all occupations and incomes, all generations and races, and all regions of the country.

More than a quarter of a million women told us that "improving pay scales" is their top priority for change. Nearly 60 percent of American women working year-round and full-time get paid less than $25,000 per year. Approximately half of all women work in traditionally female job categories such as clerical worker, nurse, teacher, librarian, and child care provider, most of which are relatively low-paying. Women of color are crowded into some of the very lowest-paying of these jobs. Few women think their wages reflect the real value of their work.

These women also told us that they want their true value in the workplace reflected in their paychecks. And pay that does not fairly reflect the value of women's contributions hurts whole families—men, women, and children!

How Women End Up with Unequal Pay

How do women end up with unequal pay? Here are a few examples:

- A woman has been turned down for numerous promotions after refusing to respond favorably to sexual advances made by her supervisor.
- A woman works as a librarian or a teacher, has a master's degree, and still does not get paid a salary she can support her children on. She has worked hard for her education, paid a lot of money for it, and thinks she is doing a very important job—but that is not what her salary says.
- A "woman's job" is paid lower than a "man's job" in the same company—a job that requires the same amount of skill, effort, and responsibility.
- A man works in a "woman's" occupation and thinks he is paid less than the men who work in "men's" occupations and have less responsibility than he does.

Over the years, working women and their organizations, including labor unions and employee associations, have campaigned to raise wages to levels that reflect the value of "women's work." Men who work in traditionally female occupations as teachers or librarians also benefit from reducing the wage gap. More importantly, the entire household benefits economically when its members receive fair pay for work of equal value.

What Is Fair Pay or Pay Equity?

Fair pay or pay equity tries to eliminate sex and race discrimination in wage-setting practices. It means equal pay for work of equal value, even when that work is different. Fair pay corrects a common practice of paying less for work performed by women. Women may perform jobs with different duties from the jobs performed by men, but if the "male" and "female" jobs are equally valuable to the employer, they should be paid comparably.

Unequal pay because of sex and race has a long history. For generations, it was legal to pay women and people of color just a fraction of what majority-group men were paid for the same job. Since 1963, the *Equal Pay Act* requires equal pay for the same work, but today about half of all employed women are in jobs that are different from those that men do. Traditional "women's work" may be undervalued in part because people think of it as a natural extension of women's family and household responsibilities and therefore not appearing to require any special or additional skills. Fair-pay advocates are currently trying to change the law so that it covers jobs that may be different from men's jobs but are still equal or equivalent. Others argue that women should simply be given greater opportunity to work less than a full-time schedule. Of course, if they choose to do so, adequate policies providing for their health and retirement should be formulated.

Part-time or at-home work is not, however, the only option. Women should be permitted to develop to their full potential, if they so choose, without the economic penalty as it currently exists, given this longstanding wage gap. While these policy issues are discussed and ultimately resolved in the appropriate forum, many steps can be taken by women and men, employers and unions to address these concerns.

What Can Be Done About Pay Inequity

Employers, unions, and you as an individual can help to address and alleviate the problem of equity in pay.

What Employers Can Do: Gender-Neutral Job Evaluation Studies. Increasingly, many employers realize that if they do not increase the pay for predominantly female jobs, they may no longer have access to a skilled work force. Many of the fastest-growing jobs in the economy are predominantly female jobs, and increasing numbers of women are entering better-paid, nontraditional jobs, which have become more accessible to them since civil rights protections became law. More employers understand the need to review their wage-setting practices to make sure they are paying their employees fairly. Job evaluation studies are one of the most useful tools available to employers,

employee associations, and unions. This is what they do:
- Job evaluation is the process by which the value of jobs is determined. It is also the cornerstone of a good fair-pay study.
- A job-evaluation plan compares all positions within one establishment, despite job dissimilarity or level in the organization. It measures accurately several factors including the inherent skill, effort, responsibility, and working conditions of each job and measures these factors for each position in the organization. Combined with analysis of job descriptions and of pay practices, these studies can identify and fix wage practices that do not reward work of equal value with equal pay.
- Employers who have conducted studies and implemented fair-pay policies within their establishments often find their system of evaluating employees improved. For example, accurate, up-to-date job descriptions can be used to develop and implement a performance-appraisal system. These descriptions also will enable the organization to establish more accurate criteria for hiring and rewarding employees. Furthermore, evaluating jobs and paying workers according to their value allows employers to attract, retain, and motivate the most competent work force, while keeping costs low enough to remain competitive.

What Unions Can Do: Negotiating Fair Pay. Hundreds of state, city, and county governments, community colleges, universities, and other employers (some private) across the United States have raised the wages of traditionally female jobs after studying the issue—often pressed to do so by a union, a women's group, or elected officials. Union participation has been an important ingredient of most fair-pay or pay-equity adjustments.

During the past twenty years, unions have increasingly opened their top ranks to full participation by women and people of color, making pay equity a higher priority. Unions have played an important role in making workers' fair-pay concerns more visible and in negotiating specific pay increases or job-classification changes across the United States. In two-thirds of the state governments that have made pay adjustments for their employees, more than half of all women workers received pay increases through these programs, according to the Institute for Women's Policy Research. More fair-pay activities have occurred in the public sector than in the private, partly because the wages and job descriptions of government employees are public information. Job evaluation studies can easily fit civil service systems. Also, laws governing collective bargaining and civil service laws and practices often refer to the importance of fair and equitable pay. In addition, elected officials control whether money is designated to narrow any wage gap found. These officials often respond to constituents who press their concerns in an organized way.

What Women Can Do: The Women's Bureau Fair Pay Clearinghouse. Most importantly, women need to understand the underlying facts so that they may develop the appropriate solutions in partnership with employers and, sometimes, with other interested parties. A good place to start is the Women's Bureau Fair Pay Clearinghouse, created to provide information to help working women and men, employers, and other organizations "improve pay scales." One working woman might be easily overwhelmed by trying to convince an employer to implement fair-pay practices by herself. Women who face this challenge can contact the Fair Pay Clearinghouse and through it make contact with other organizations that can help.

You can call, write, or visit the Women's Bureau website on the Internet to get information on:

- wages and traditionally female occupations;
- how women of different races, ethnic origins, ages, and educational backgrounds are paid;
- resource organizations, including associations in your occupational category (such as nurses or librarians), labor unions, and business organizations in your state and nationwide that are active on fair-pay issues; and
- pay adjustments made by employers across the country.

Contacting the Fair Pay Clearinghouse will give you the right tools to find out what the facts are, to know your rights, and to learn what works from pioneering efforts by organizations committed to working women.

> *"Women's economic position continues to improve while men's is beginning to decline."*

Claims That Women Face Discrimination in the Workplace Are Exaggerated

Elizabeth Fox-Genovese

Elizabeth Fox-Genovese is the author of Feminism Is Not the Story of My Life: *How Today's Feminist Elite Has Lost Touch with the Real Concerns of Women*, from which the following viewpoint is excerpted. In this viewpoint, Fox-Genovese contends that feminists' assertions that women are treated unequally within the workplace are exaggerated. In reality, she writes, women are entering the workforce in rapid numbers and their average income is rising steadily. Although some women may face workplace discrimination, evidence shows that middle- and upper-class women are prospering. If feminists truly want to help women, Fox-Genovese claims, they should focus their attention on the economic inequalities that make it difficult for poor working women to support themselves and their families.

As you read, consider the following questions:

1. How does Fox-Genovese support her claim that the 1980s were not a period of backlash for working women?
2. According to the author, how does discrimination affect women in the workplace?
3. What is true equality within the workplace, as stated by the author?

From the start, pay equity—equal pay for equal work—has ranked as a major feminist issue and, of all feminist issues, has spoken the most directly to ordinary women—and men. "Fifty-nine cents on the dollar" swiftly captured the popular imagination. And from 1960 to 1980, it captured the reality of women's experience. Today, it does not. By 1991, the fifty-nine cents had become seventy cents for women in general—an amazing improvement for a brief period. Equal pay for equal work is no longer the main problem and probably will soon be no problem at all. The real problem is how little difference the closing of that gap makes in the lives of many women, whose earnings have become more important to their own support and the support of their families.

When feminists first called attention to the inequality of men's and women's earnings, they seemed to assume that if women made as much as men they would be economically self-sufficient, if not comfortable. But equal pay for equal work always meant precisely that: For women to earn the same as men, they must hold the same jobs and must hold them for the same amount of time. As we all now know, this is not a scenario that easily includes motherhood. Beyond the difficulties of juggling employment and motherhood lies the reality of our economy. Just because a woman who works at McDonald's earns as much as a male coworker with the same amount of experience does not mean that she earns enough to support herself and one or two children. . . .

Different Circumstances for Different Groups of Women

We cannot possibly understand what has been happening to women's earnings if we group all women together. "Fifty-nine cents on the dollar" reflected the average experience of all women in the labor force no matter what their age or education or how much of their lives they had worked. Typically, older women had always earned less than the men of their age, especially if they left the labor force or worked part-time when their children were young. They rarely had the opportunities to enter lucrative careers and professions that young women enjoy today. Poor women still do not have the appropriate education. So the average improvement in women's earnings disguises the radically different circumstances of different groups.

While some groups of women saw little or no improvement in their earnings, others leapfrogged into the highest brackets. The real story concerns which women won and which women lost or barely held steady in the new employment lottery. In general, younger women have been the big winners, and today young full-time women workers are earning 90 percent or more of what their male colleagues earn. Of this group, the women with the most education have done the best of all. Tellingly, the more education a woman has, the more likely she is to seek employment—and, apparently, to find it. As of 1992, women held almost half of all managerial and professional positions. Education, enhanced by affirmative action, thus helped women to move into the white collar and managerial sectors that were previously dominated by men. But women who have entered nontraditional occupations that do not require as much education have also done remarkably well, although they have frequently faced serious challenges in getting their coworkers to accept them.

Women who become mechanics and skilled repair workers, like women who become welders, engineers, law enforcement officers, or firefighters, still enter a man's world. The plus is that they are taking up occupations that offer reasonably high wages. The minus is that many of their male coworkers offer them a less than cordial welcome. Geraldine Walker, a ship scaler and the only black woman supervisor at her shipyard, likes working in the yards, even though she believes her work contributed to her divorce. "I'm a lot stronger now than when I started in the yards. I don't doubt now that I can take care of myself. Financially, emotionally, I'm more confident." So, to earn their wages they not only have to do their jobs, they frequently have to contend with subtle and not-so-subtle forms of harassment. It should come as no surprise that many of the men with whom they work do not think that they belong there. Marge Kirk, who works as a concrete truck driver, remembers putting up with a lot of sexual innuendoes, especially from the dispatcher who was her supervisor. "It takes a lot of energy just to stand

37

your ground—balancing male egos with your right to sur- vive." But she "wanted to be a good truck driver," and "somehow I survived." Other women have done the same as mechanics, skilled repair workers, security guards, police, or firefighters, and the wages of women in these occupations have been steadily rising. But working in "male" occupations does not alone explain the general improvement in women's earnings; secretaries, who are mainly women, have enjoyed the biggest increase of all.

The numbers challenge feminism's picture of the Reagan and Bush years as a period of backlash against women. The 1980s did very well by many women. They did not do well by others. The many women in service occupations such as food preparation or day care and in typically "female" occu- pations such as manicurist or beautician did badly, and they may soon do worse, especially those with children to sup- port. But men from similar backgrounds, with similar edu- cations, are doing no better. If anything, women are more likely than men to pursue the education that our modern economy demands. According to the Census Bureau, the number of women who enter the labor force with a college degree is rising one and one-half times as rapidly as the number of men. The continuing decline of occupational segregation is producing more and more direct competition between women and men for jobs and wages. This direct competition is new, and it is pushing down men's wages. During the years of the so-called backlash, women's average income grew by almost 30 percent, while the average in- come of men actually declined slightly.

Women's Economic Position Is Improving

No, women in general are still not doing as well as men in general. Yes, some men do resent the gains that women have made and do their best to prevent them from making more. It should not be difficult to understand that direct competition between women and men for employment and wages could result in men's resentment of women—and even a backlash. But no backlash has prevented significant numbers of upscale white women from prospering. More important, even while most women still do less well than men in absolute terms, women's economic position continues to improve while men's is beginning to decline. The gap is steadily closing.

So why, in the face of improvement, do feminists continue to stress discrimination? One may only assume that, understandably, they resent not having advanced as rapidly or as far as they had hoped. Each of us sees the world through the lens of her own life. Naomi Wolf, who acknowledges that women have made terrific gains in many areas, continues to protest, probably with good reason, their disadvantage in the media—her own world. Women who have butted their heads against the notorious corporate "glass ceiling" feel the same about theirs. Knowing themselves to be as talented and accomplished (often more so) than the men with whom they work, they find it tempting to blame their troubles upon men who are determined to keep them down. In this frame of mind, they are unlikely to be impressed by reminders of the extraordinary improvement in the situation of women like themselves.

Discrimination Against Women in the Workplace

We should not lightly dismiss men's persisting determination to continue to control the workplace. Most successful women in business or the professions will at least privately complain of a male network that they simply cannot crack. The workings of these networks are subtle, private, and elusive, consisting in conversations over a drink or a game of golf at which women just happen not to be present. Sexual harassment, even in its mildest form of passing remarks, remains a problem. As women have entered the labor force in ever greater numbers, their perception of discrimination has increased. And college women perceive more discrimination than women with less education. Meanwhile, the women and men who have the least chance to become executives—nonwhites or those with only a grade school education—are the most likely to believe that a woman has as good a chance as a man to become one. Doubtless, some men do resent female competition, but others benefit directly from the improvement in women's earnings through their wives, daughters, and partners. And increasing numbers of working-class as well as middle-class men are making a successful effort to come to terms with their women coworkers.

In fairness to the feminist elite, it is clear that as of the 1990s women still have not made significant inroads on the top executive positions. In 1991, when women accounted for almost half the labor force and, depending upon the estimate, 25 to 40 percent of all managers, they held less, by some counts much less, than 10 percent of the top executive positions. Variations in job classifications make statistical precision difficult, but during the past ten years, women have been making dramatic gains in upper management. Some companies have let it be known that women only need apply for some of their top jobs. Even so, the only women who are faring better than the men of their own group are black women professionals, who, as of 1994, outnumbered black male professionals by nearly two to one in the 38,000 companies that report to the Equal Employment Opportunity Commission.

Women Are Succeeding in the Workplace

Women who want full-time careers today and are willing to give all they've got are the big-time winners in modern feminism. The wage gap in the United States was down to 2 percent in 1997 among women and men who were willing to make similar life choices and compete equally for the same kind of work, according to statistics published by the Independent Women's Forum, a conservative women's lobbying organization in Washington. These are women who earn 98 percent of what men earn, who are between the ages 27 and 33 and who have never had a child.

That's not the only good news. Women are running their businesses in record numbers, generating jobs for men as well as women. Feminists who look only at the victim status of women are looking through the wrong end of the telescope.

Suzanne Fields, *Insight*, June 29, 1998.

In 1992, *Business Week* surveyed four hundred female managers, only to find that they divided equally among those who believed that corporate America was doing "somewhat better" in hiring and promoting women and those who believed that the rate of progress was slowing. The main difficulty in assessing any of these numbers or even the responses to them is that the numbers themselves are so small. If a company that has one woman in a senior executive position adds a second, it will have increased the percentage of women by 100 percent. If its one woman retires or leaves and is replaced with a man, it will be left with no senior women executives at all. These are indeed circumstances designed to provoke bitterness and outrage, and they are circumstances upon which feminists have readily focused. After all, does not the low number of women at the top of the corporate ladder confirm the prevalence of blatant sexism? Doubtless it does. The rage and frustration of the women caught in it should surprise no one. But the corporate world that still treats women shabbily is beginning to treat many men even worse. For between 1982 and 1992, when men lost a net 93,000 management jobs, women gained a net 520,000 management jobs. Under these conditions, men are easily tempted to see a sexism in reverse. What, in fact, they are seeing is a ruthlessness that knows neither sex nor race in its concern for the bottom line of its ledgers and need to appease one or another political lobby. Sometimes women are simply taking over men's jobs; sometimes the men's jobs are eliminated entirely, and the women are hired for new jobs at lower pay.

The Wage Gap Is on the Verge of Extinction

In principle, Americans have long favored paying women the same as men for the same work. As early as 1976, two thirds also approved of working wives, with the strongest support coming from the upscale and the young. And in 1982, when women were entering the labor force in growing numbers, the vast majority, especially those with the most education, believed that women should enjoy the same job opportunities as men. Today, virtually everyone agrees that women and men who do the same work should receive the same pay. But support for working women in principle does not necessarily mean support in practice. And even people with the best of intentions often find it difficult to act on their beliefs. Continuing inequalities persist and should not be brushed aside. The essential point nonetheless remains: The gap between men and women in wages and salaries is on the verge of extinction. The one exception is the most important case of all, namely mothers. But their needs do not rank at the top of anyone's agenda.

No one can pretend that women and men started out on an equal—or level—playing field. Thirty years ago men monopolized the best positions and the highest incomes throughout our economy. Today, women are claiming a steadily increasing share of both positions and incomes, but women as a group have still not attained equality with men as a group. Nor, as many women are quick to point out, have specific women always attained parity with specific men where parity seems appropriate. But the average of all women and the cases of specific women both obscure what may well be more important: The economic revolution that has drawn women into the labor force has transformed our economy, widening the gap between social classes and races but narrowing the gap between women and men within classes and races.

Feminism has ridden the crest of an economic wave that is pushing a disquieting number of Americans into a poverty from which they have little hope of escape. The same economic wave has been assaulting the security and self-confidence of many middle-class families, largely through the declining value of wages and the loss of male jobs. Between 1973 and 1992, the average wages for the bottom 60 percent of male workers fell by 20 percent, and among young full-time male workers (ages eighteen to twenty-four) the percentage earning less than $12,195 a year jumped from 18 to 40—that is, it more than doubled. For comparable young women, the percentage went from 29 to 48. These stark figures draw a bleak picture for everyone: First, young women have consistently earned less than young men; second, the gap between the earnings of young women and those of young men has narrowed; and third, the numbers of both young men and young women who have poor prospects for earning a decent living has skyrocketed. Meanwhile, the richest Americans have increased their numbers and grown richer.

In this new and threatening economic world, two incomes are not just better than one: For most Americans, they are necessary. It is a world in which many, if not most, women must work, struggling to raise their children as best they can.

It is a world in which the woman worker is a mother and often is poor because she is a mother. Feminism has been inclined to focus on professional and managerial women and to blame men for the disadvantages that women still suffer. But the young upscale women on whom official feminism focuses are doing remarkably well, and in the measure that they still have not attained full equality with men it is normally because of their responsibilities to children. Yet the economic revolution that has brought this group of women to an unprecedented independence and prosperity has condemned others to insecurity and even poverty.

What Does Equality Mean?

What, in such a world, does equality mean? So long as women bear children, they will not be identical to men—and hence not equal to them. The measures of mathematical equality have little to do with the fabric of human lives. They have everything to do with the size of paychecks, whether equal or not. The differences between paychecks have more to do with the differences between social classes—and increasingly the education that, more than anything else today, determines class membership—than with the differences between the sexes. Within classes, differences between women and men persist, although they are steadily lessening. And, in the end, the best explanation for them remains women's ability to bear children—the inequality that no amount of social policy can erase. Social policy can ease the consequences of that inequality. But it is unlikely to accomplish even that much until we replace the feminist quest for an illusory equality with compassionate attention to the lives most women actually live.

"Every day, . . . four or five women die in the United States at the hands of their current or former husbands or boyfriends."

Violence Against Women Is a Serious Problem

Ann Jones

In the following viewpoint, Ann Jones states that violence against women—especially within domestic situations—has reached epidemic proportions. In fact, according to FBI estimates, every year men murder three thousand wives and girlfriends. In order to protect women from male violence, Jones asserts, the battered women's movement must work to ensure that batterers suffer social and legal consequences for their behavior. Jones is the author of a variety of books on women, battering, and criminal justice, including *Next Time, She'll Be Dead: Battering and How to Stop It.*

As you read, consider the following questions:

1. According to the Statistics Canada study cited by Jones, how serious is the problem of violence against women?
2. In the author's opinion, what mistaken beliefs do people have about battering men?
3. What evidence does Jones offer that batterers suffer no social or legal consequences for their behavior?

Excerpted from "Battering: Who's Going to Stop It?" by Ann Jones, in *Bad Girls, Good Girls: Women, Sex, and Power in the Nineties* (New Brunswick: Rutgers University Press, 1996) edited by Nan Bauer and Donna Perry. Reprinted by permission of Ann Jones.

Recently, at Mount Holyoke College—the oldest women's college in the country—the student newspaper carried the front page headline: "Domestic Violence on the Rise." Reported cases of "domestic" violence were increasing all across the country, according to student reporter Gretchen Hitchner—and on the Mount Holyoke campus as well. "There are five or six students on campus who have obtained stay-away orders," Hitchner reported.

Beyond the boundaries of the campus, the statistics grew much worse. Statewide, in Massachusetts in 1991, a woman was murdered by a current or former husband or boyfriend every twenty days. By 1993, such a murder occurred once every eight days. Among the dead: Tara Hartnett, a twenty-one-year-old senior psychology major at the nearby University of Massachusetts at Amherst. In February 1993, Tara Hartnett had obtained a restraining order against James Cyr, Jr., her former boyfriend and the father of her eleven-month-old daughter. In March, when Hartnett's roommates were away on spring break, Cyr broke in, stabbed Hartnett, set the house on fire, and left her to die of smoke inhalation.

"Incidents" like the murder of Tara Hartnett happen all the time. Every day, in fact, four or five women die in the United States at the hands of their current or former husbands or boyfriends. But recently feminists (like me) who call attention to these crimes have been taking a lot of heat for perpetuating the image of women as "victims." Critics charge that "victim feminists" exaggerate the dangers women face in male violence. Katie Roiphe, for example, suggests in her book *The Morning After* that most alleged cases of date rape involve nothing more than second thoughts by daylight after bad sex the night before. Battering, according to the critics, is nothing that any woman with moderate self-esteem and a bus token can't escape. What prevents women from exercising our full female power and strength, some say, is not male violence but the *fear* of violence induced by fuddy-duddy feminists who see all women as victims.

Real Violence or Hysterical Perceptions?

Could it be true that the apparent crime wave against women, on campus and off, is only a delusion of paranoid radical feminists? Is it real violence that keeps women down, or only feminists' hysterical perceptions that hamper us?

In Canada, where the same questions were raised, Statistics Canada attempted to find out by interviewing 12,300 women nationwide in the most comprehensive study of violence against women ever undertaken. The results were worse than expected. They showed violence against women to be far more common than earlier, smaller scale studies had indicated. They revealed that more than half of Canadian women (51 percent) have been physically or sexually assaulted at least once in their adult lives. And more than half of those women said they'd been attacked by dates, boyfriends, husbands, friends, family members, or other men familiar to them. One in ten Canadian women, or one million, had been attacked in the past year.

These figures apply only to Canada, but considering that the United States is a more violent culture all around, it's unlikely that women in the United States are any safer from attack. In fact, battering alone is now the single leading cause of injury to women in the United States. A million women every year visit physicians and hospital emergency rooms for treatment of battering injuries. The National Centers for Disease Control identify battering as a leading cause of the spread of HIV and AIDS, as countless batterers force "their" women into unprotected sex. The American Medical Association reports that 38 percent of obstetric patients are battered during pregnancy, and studies name battering during pregnancy a cause of birth defects and infant mortality.

Survivors confirm that a man often begins to batter during a woman's first pregnancy, when she is most vulnerable and least able to pack up and move. Marie's husband, a lawyer, beat her so severely during her seventh month that she went into labor. He then ripped out the phone, locked her in a second-floor bedroom, and left the house. She barely survived, and the little boy she bore that day has always been small and frail. Carol miscarried after her husband knocked her down and kicked her repeatedly in the belly. He threatened to kill her if she tried to leave. When she became pregnant again, he beat her again, saying "I'm going to kill that baby and you, too." Instead, she killed him with his own gun and was sentenced to twenty years in prison, where she bore her child and gave it up for adoption. Jean left her husband after he repeatedly punched her in the belly while she was pregnant. Later, when a doctor told Jean that her daughter had epilepsy, he asked if Jean had suffered a fall or an "accident" of any kind during pregnancy. Now that her daughter is in college and still suffering seizures, Jean says, "I only lived with that man for a year, but he casts his shadow over every day of my life, and my daughter's, too."

The Reality of Male Violence

Millions of women live with such consequences of male violence, but it's not surprising that many choose another way out. Battering is cited as a contributing factor in a quarter of all suicide attempts by women, and half of all suicide attempts by black women. At least 50 percent of homeless women and children in the United States are in flight from male violence. Only a few years ago the FBI reported that in the United States a man beat a woman every eighteen seconds. By 1989, the figure was fifteen seconds. Now it's twelve.

Some people take those facts and statistics at face value to mean that male violence is on the rise; while others argue that what's increasing is merely the *reporting* of violence. But no matter how you interpret the numbers, it's clear that male violence is not going *down*.

As crime statistics go, homicide figures are most likely to be accurate, for the simple reason that homicides produce corpses—hard to hide and easy to count. Homicide figures all across the country—like those in Massachusetts—indicate so clearly that violence against women is on the rise that some sociologists have coined a new term for a common crime: "femicide." The FBI estimates that every year men murder about three thousand wives and girlfriends. The conclusion is inescapable: male violence against women is *real*. And it is widespread.

Battering Affects Young, Single Women

Such violence was once thought of as the plague of married women, but battering, like date rape, affects young, single women as well. In its recent study, Statistics Canada found

Statistics on the Murder of Women Fifteen Years and Older by Relationship: 1976–1987

Relationship	# Women Murdered	Percentage	Percentage in Known Relationships
Husband/common law	11,236	22.81	33.10
Other Family	2,937	5.96	8.65
Other intimates, e.g. friend, date, cohabiting relationship	5,318	10.80	15.67
Acquaintances	9,930	20.16	29.26
Strangers	4,521	9.18	13.32
Undetermined (assume strangers but very few serial killers)	15,320	31.10	
Total	49,262	100.01	100.00

James A. Mercy, "Men, Women, and Murder: Gender-Specific Differences in Rates of Fatal Violence and Victimization," *Journal of Trauma*.

that a disproportionate number of women reporting physical or sexual assault were young. Women ages eighteen to twenty-four were more than twice as likely as older women to report violence in the year preceding the study; 27 percent of them had been attacked in the past year. In the United States, the first study of "premarital abuse," conducted in 1985, reported that one in five college students was the victim of "physical aggression," ranging from slapping and hitting to "more life threatening violence." When a guy who'd had too much to drink offered Sarah a ride home from a fraternity party, she turned him down and advised him not to drive. He waited for her outside and beat her up—to "teach the bitch a lesson," he said. Susan went home for her first break from college and told her hometown boyfriend that she wanted to date at school. In response, he deliberately pulled out clumps of her hair, broke her arm, and drove her car into a tree. After Bonnie broke up with a possessive guy she'd been dating at college, he sneaked into her home at night and smashed in her head with a hatchet. Typically, guys like this think they're *entitled* to get their way, by any means necessary. Resorting to violence seems justified to them. They think they've done nothing wrong—or at least no more than she *asked* for.

Even high school boys are acting out the macho myth. A study of white middle-class high school juniors and seniors found that roughly one in four had some experience of dating violence, either as victim or perpetrator. In another study one in three teenage girls reported being subjected to physical violence by a date. After reviewing many such studies of high school and college students, Barrie Levy, author of *In Love and In Danger: A Teen's Guide to Breaking Free of Abusive Relationships*, reports that "an average of twenty-eight percent of the students experienced violence in a dating relationship. That is more than one in every four students." Male counselors who work with wife beaters confirm that many older batterers first began to use violence as teenagers, against their dates.

That doesn't mean that violence against young women is just "kid's stuff." According to the FBI, 20 percent of women murdered in the United States are between the ages of fifteen and twenty-four. Recently a high school boy in Texas shot his girlfriend for being "unfaithful," and for good measure he killed her best friend, too. Former police officer Barbara Arrighi, who has witnessed increased date rape, battering, and stalking among college students as assistant director for public safety at Mount Holyoke College, bluntly sums up the situation: "Anyone who doesn't believe America has a serious problem with violence against young women," she says, "is living in Lalaland.". . .

The Battering Man

To find an explanation for the high rate of male violence against young women, we have to look to the source: to men. Many people still mistakenly believe that batterers are somehow different from ordinary men—that they are "crazy" men with short fuses who "lose control" of themselves and blow up, especially when under the influence of drink or drugs. But those who counsel batterers say that just the reverse is true: the battering man is perfectly *in* control of himself—and of the woman he batters. That, after all, is the purpose of battering. A man—of any age—threatens, intimidates, abuses, and batters a woman to make her do what he wants. It works. He gets his way, and as a bonus he gets a heady rush of experiencing his own power. As one reformed eighteen-year-old guy put it: "I enjoyed intimidating people." David Adams, director of Emerge, a Boston counseling program for batterers, points out that the same man who says he "loses control" of his temper with "his" woman will be perfectly calm when the police arrive. "Clearly he knows what he's doing," Adams says. "He's making rational choices about how to act with whom—on the basis of what he can get away with."

It's likely, then, that young women—even young women "in love"—get battered for the same reason older women get battered. Namely, they have minds of their own. They want to do what they want. Battered women are often mistakenly thought of as "passive" or "helpless" because some of them look that way *after* they've been beaten into submission and made hostage to terror. Their inability to escape is the *result* of battering, not its cause. According to one study, three out of four battering victims are actually single or separated women trying to get free of men who won't let them go. They are not merely victims; they are the resistance. But they are almost entirely on their own.

Protecting Women from Violence

How can we help women get free of this violence? That's the question that survivors of battering and their advocates have been grappling with for twenty years. And they've done a phenomenal job. Never before in history has there been such an organization of crime victims united to rescue other victims and prevent further crimes. Although battered women's shelters are still so overburdened that they must turn away more women than they take in, they have provided safe haven over the years for millions of women and their children. Undoubtedly, they have saved thousands of lives.

In addition, the battered women's movement has brought battering out of the private household and into the spotlight of public debate. There it has raised a much harder question: how can we make men stop their violence? To that end, the battered women's movement has pushed for—and achieved—big changes in legislation, public policy, and law enforcement. The Violence Against Women Act, passed by Congress in 1994, is only one recent example. This bill correctly considers male violence against women as a violation of women's civil rights and provides a wide range of legal remedies for women.

But what's needed is a national campaign to go after the men at fault. Experts such as Susan Schechter, author of *Women and Male Violence*, say that men continue to use violence to get their way *because they can*. Nobody stops them. There's no reason for a man who uses violence to change his behavior unless he begins to suffer some real consequences, some punishment that drives home strong social and legal prohibitions against battering. In the short run, the most effective way to protect women and children, save lives, and cut down violence is to treat assault as the crime it is: to arrest batterers and send them to jail.

The Need for More Stringent Laws

Usually, that's not what happens. Right now, most batterers suffer *no* social or legal consequences at all for their criminal behavior. Although police in most states and localities are now authorized to arrest batterers, many police departments still don't enforce the law. If police do make arrests, prosecutors commonly fail to prosecute. And if batterers are convicted, judges often release them—or worse, order them into marital counseling *with* the women they've assaulted. Many men are required to attend a few weekly sessions of a therapeutic support group where they shoot the breeze with other batterers, after which their crime is erased from the record books. (Counselors like David Adams who lead such groups are the first to say that the groups don't work.) One 1991 study found that among assaultive men arrested, prosecuted, convicted, and sentenced, less than 1 percent (0.9 percent) served any time in jail. The average batterer taken into custody by police is held less than two hours. He walks away laughing at his victim and at the police as well.

Even men convicted of near-fatal attacks upon their girl-friends or wives are likely to draw light sentences or be released on probation with plenty of opportunity to finish the job. The husband of Burnadette Barnes, for example, shot her in the head while she slept, served three months in prison for the offense, and was released to threaten her again. Desperate, Burnadette Barnes hired a man to kill her husband. She was convicted of murder and conspiracy to murder and sentenced to life in prison.

In Michigan, police officer Clarence Ratliff shot and killed his estranged wife, Carol Irons, who incidentally was the youngest woman ever appointed to the Michigan bench. (As a judge she was known to treat domestic violence cases seriously.) When the police tried to arrest Ratliff, he squeezed off a few wild shots before he surrendered. For killing his wife, Ratliff got ten to fifteen years; for shooting at the cops, two life terms plus some additional shorter terms for using a firearm.

Such cases make clear that in the scales of American justice men weigh more than women. Assaulting a man is a serious crime, but assaulting a woman or even killing her— well, that's not so bad.

We can do better. Thanks to the battered women's movement, we now know that any social, economic, or political development that counteracts sexism and promotes sex equality helps in the long run to eliminate violence by reducing the power men hold, individually and institutionally, over women. We now know that all the institutions to which battered women and children are likely to turn for help— hospitals, mental health facilities, social welfare services, child protective services, police departments, civil and criminal courts, schools, churches—must join a *concerted* effort to prevent violence before it occurs and stop it when it does. They must stand ready to defend the constitutional right that belongs to all women—(though no one ever speaks of it): the right to be free from bodily harm.

> *"From rape redefinitions to feminist theory on the 'patriarchy,' victimization has become the . . . moral to be found in every feminist story."*

Feminists Have Overstated the Problem of Violence Against Women

Rene Denfeld

In the viewpoint that follows, Rene Denfeld argues that feminists have dramatically exaggerated the scope and seriousness of male violence in their attempt to prove that women are "victimized" by men. The "victim mythology" adopted by feminists conveys the message that men will always be predators and women will always be their prey—a message that frightens women and unfairly demonizes men. Denfeld is the author of *The New Victorians: A Young Woman's Challenge to the Old Feminist Order*, from which this viewpoint is selected.

As you read, consider the following questions:

1. What evidence does Denfeld offer to support her view that feminists exaggerate the incidence of violence against women?
2. As stated by Denfeld, how do today's feminists portray women?
3. In the author's opinion, why is the "victim mythology" appealing to many women?

Women today are constantly confronted with the dangers of being born female. Magazine articles, newspaper accounts, and feminist literature all report chilling statistics: that at least one in four women will be raped, that as many as one in four girls are victims of incest, and that nearly all men—if given the chance—would sexually force themselves on women. To be female today sounds like a terrifying proposition: Surrounded by a society of male predators, we are constantly in danger of being attacked by friends, lovers, husbands, and strangers. Many of these attacks are said to occur on dates, by men we trust. Others, we are told, will happen in the office, on the streets, in our homes.

Naturally, we are frightened. To protect ourselves we constrain our lives, viewing every relationship as if it were a dark alley filled with menacing shadows. It would be too easy, it seems, to become that one woman in four. "It's horrible thinking of yourself as vulnerable, that each time you walk out your door some violent HE may be waiting," writes Marcia Ann Gillespie, *Ms.* magazine's executive editor, in the September/October 1990 issue.

That the man you meet for dinner tonight may assume he has unlimited rights to the use of your body. That the man you know as warm, funny, and kind may one day turn around and slam his fist into your skull, throw you against a wall or down a flight of stairs. That your husband, lover, son, or brother may be a terrorist in waiting."

Her fears seem backed up by the numbers. We are told that almost nine out of ten women will be assaulted or harassed.

But where do these terrifying statistics come from and what are they based on? Not from government figures or reliable studies, nor are they based on legal definitions of sexual assault. In fact, they come from just two surveys conducted by separate feminist researchers, Diana E.H. Russell and Mary P. Koss. Their surveys . . . reveal scientific flaws. Russell and Koss have included everything from consensual sex to obscene phone calls in their figures on rape and sexual abuse. Their numbers have little to do with what most people call rape, and everything to do with a new feminist agenda.

By promoting these skewed studies, current feminists promote a new status for women: that of the victim. In their view, those women who have been sexually assaulted are not the only ones deeply traumatized. Joining them are women who have experienced wolf whistles, off-color jokes, glances from men, and even the most loving of sexual relationships. All these things, according to today's feminists, are forms of rape. "Rape, as we have defined it, is any sexual intimacy, whether by direct physical contact or not, that is forced on one person by another," assert Andrea Medea and Kathleen Thompson in *Against Rape*, which is assigned to students attending introductory women's studies courses at the State University of New York at Albany. Considered radical when published in the seventies, this tract joins many more current works presented as mainstream feminism to women today. As examples of rape, the book includes "whistles and comments" from men on the street, "familiar" pats from coworkers, and "the obnoxious drunk at the next table."

And this is far from just an American phenomenon—feminists in England and Canada, among other countries, also push extreme redefinitions of rape. As English feminist Liz Kelly explains in her 1988 book, *Surviving Sexual Violence*,

> Sexual violence includes *any physical, visual, verbal or sexual act experienced by the woman or girl, at the time or later, as a threat, invasion or assault, that has the effect of hurting her or degrading her and/or takes away her ability to control intimate contact.*

Just what does this mean? Kelly goes on to include "leering," "whistles," "sexual joking," "being touched by strangers on the streets," and "unexplained silent phone calls" as forms of sexual violence.

The Bitter Reality of Rape

Rape is a brutal and ugly crime. The victims of sexual crimes deserve both legal help and community support for the trauma they've experienced. We need to confront the bitter reality that—according to the FBI—almost half of all reported rape cases (47 percent in 1990) are not cleared through arrest or other means. As long as the arrest rate is this low, too many rapists stay free to rape again. We need to put pressure on law-enforcement agencies to catch and incarcerate rapists. We need to create and better fund police sexual-assault units, we need to increase sentences for rape, we need to institute more treatment programs for sex offenders in prisons, we need to improve the way rape victims are treated by the courts, and we need to help victims put their lives back together.

But few of today's feminists are pushing for these goals. "Programs and strategies to combat rape are not a priority on the federal, state or local level," former Congresswoman Elizabeth Holtzman stated in the May 1990 issue of *McCall's*. "It is a serious failure of political leadership." Part of this failure must rest on the shoulders of feminists, who should be putting pressure on politicians to make rape a priority—one of the functions of the movement has always been to offer viable strategies and programs on women's issues and then push to see they are implemented. For the most part, the women's movement gives little more than lip service to legislation and legal help for the real victims of crime. It is true that NOW [the National Organization for Women] supports the Violence Against Women Act (a bill that would increase funding for rape prevention and better fund sexual-assault prosecution), that feminist rape crisis centers often push for more government financing, and that activists in some cities train police in rape awareness. But in the places young women encounter feminism, these kinds of actions are given scant attention. Instead, while feminists focus heavily on victimization and assault, little discussion is paid to just what women can do to remedy the problem effectively.

That's because for many of today's feminists, lobbying efforts are viewed as a worthless Band-Aid for the deeper problem: men. To work with men, even on behalf of rape victims, is a betrayal of feminism. "While some feminists have demanded state recognition of and action against male sexual violence, the ensuing response often severely compromises feminist values," writes feminist Jill Radford, coeditor of the 1992 book *Femicide: The Politics of Woman Killing*. Why? Because some victim support programs "ensure these women will not reject men."

And that rejection will be assured only if women realize they are a powerless class of victims. By redefining rape to include a ludicrously broad range of experiences, many current feminists are trying to redefine what it means to be a woman.

Rather than strong and self-reliant, today's feminists would portray women as weak and oppressed. Instead of being in control of our lives, they say we are at the mercy of a culture dominated by rapists. If consensual sex can count as rape, then most women are victims. If wolf whistles, glances, and jokes are sexual assaults, then many of us are raped on a near-daily basis. The chances are we cannot leave our homes without being attacked, and we cannot stay in our homes without experiencing rape from someone we thought we loved.

Victim Mythology

This is victim mythology. From rape redefinitions to feminist theory on the "patriarchy," victimization has become the subtext of the movement, the moral to be found in every feminist story. Together, these stories form a feminist mythology in which a singular female subject is created: woman as a helpless, violated, and oppressed victim. Victim mythology says that men will always be predators and women will always be their prey. It is a small place to live, a place that forgets strength, capability, trust, and hope. It is a place that tells women that there is really no way out. And it is a place that—instead of empowering women to change—teaches us paralyzing fear. Like other mythologies, victim mythology reduces the complexity of human interaction to grossly oversimplified mythical tales, a one-note song, where the message of the story becomes so important that fiction not only triumphs over fact but the realities of women's experiences are dismissed and derided when they conflict with the accepted female image.

And it is a mythology that harkens back to the mid to late 1800s and early 1900s, when women were also constantly portrayed as pure, dainty, and powerless. "The purity of women," wrote the author of *What Women Should Know* in 1873, "is the everlasting barrier against which the tides of man's sensual nature surge." For Victorians, the purity of women was only a weak barrier against the surging tides of male "nature." In fact, they believed it was women's destiny to be victimized through sex—a burdensome obligation for married women and a fate worse than death for single women. As long as sex existed, rape was inevitable. . . .

Men as Demons, Women as Innocents

There is nothing new or radical in this current feminist portrayal of men and women. It is simply a new twist on an old favorite: men as wicked demons with sex on the brain, women as defenseless, chaste innocents in need of protection. And the media has gone for this view whole hog. In a nostalgic tone, the September 1989 *Good Housekeeping* recalls the days of "a different, gentler campus life in which men and women lived in separate dorms and adhered to curfews." "'Does he make suggestive remarks or tell off-color jokes just to make you uncomfortable?'" the September 4, 1992, issue of *Woman's Day* quotes a University of Florida rape prevention director. Watch out girls, "'Those are red flags. Sexual assault may be ahead.'" A January 1992 *Cosmo* article concludes that the "old-fashioned advice moms have been giving daughters for generations" is the best policy for dating: "Don't allow yourself to be alone with him."

Even otherwise feminist-thinking magazines have fallen for this antifeminist view. In a May 1992 article on date rape, *Glamour* offers "a few cautions about going out with men and getting physical with them." Women are advised to watch for assault clues, such as men who buy them drinks: "Men *try* to get women drunk; it's the means to a very specific end." But above all, *Glamour* makes it clear that hanky-panky is a good way to get raped. "Should you be kissing, hugging and/or touching when you start feeling uncomfortable, his mind is likely to have fogged over somewhat," the article declares. A sexually aroused man is uncontrollable; "A man in heat is, well, a man in heat," or, as Victorian writers put it, a beast. . . .

Those who remember Germaine Greer might think that feminists would be up in arms over articles such as these. But from the current feminist front, there is only silence. It is the silence of assent. In fact, the idea that women's equality has generated more sexual violence (by placing women at greater risk) has gained popularity throughout the women's movement. "We see this escalation of violence against females as part of a male backlash against feminism," Diana Russell and Jane Caputi wrote in a September/October 1990 article for *Ms.* that identifies everything from "forced heterosexuality" to "cosmetic surgery" as part of a conspiratorial "reign of sexist terror comparable in magnitude, intensity, and intent to the persecution, torture, and annihilation of women as witches from the 14th to 17th centuries in Europe." Undoubtedly, victim mythology is appealing to many women. In a time when AIDS and venereal diseases are cause for concern, when women are still taught to have mixed feelings about sex and when college students are facing important and difficult decisions about their own sexuality, a theory that paints all men as rapists and all women as helpless victims can gain converts. It's a simple answer to confusing questions. And let's be honest. Seeing ourselves as victims is often far easier than taking responsibility for those aspects of our lives we can control, whether by telling a guy who leers at us to bug off instead of feeling helplessly violated or by acknowledging that even if we regret it the next day, consensual sex is still consensual sex—and that if we aren't threatened or incapacitated, we must take responsibility for our own decisions. A victim status based on an ideal of chaste womanhood can be deeply appealing, not only because it dismisses the responsibility of the power we do have but because it fits into comforting societal views of femininity: fragility, sexlessness, and helplessness are often still rewarded, while frank sexuality is condemned. The woman who says, "He talked me into it" after having consensual sex is still seen as a good girl. The young woman who says, "I invited him up to my place; we got naked and had a blast" is often still deemed a slut.

But accepting victim mythology is not without a price. To accept feminist redefinitions of rape, women must accept that even when they say yes, feminists will say no. They have to accept that men cannot be trusted. And they have to accept that, from the bedroom to the boardroom, equality with men means a greater likelihood of assault. Since male glances and jokes are assaultive, working with men will only encourage rape. Since women's rights have caused a "backlash" of violence, fighting on behalf of equal pay and job advancement in a man's world will only increase the occurrence of rape. Since heterosexual sex is a violation, fighting for better birth control and national day-care programs will only promote the practice of assault, taking place, as Robin Morgan insists, in bedrooms across America that are "settings for nightly rape." This twisted logic is one reason why young women, and women of all ages, reject today's women's movement. We have been told that feminism no longer stands for equality; it stands for things that once were considered the antithesis of feminism: helplessness, hysteria, paralyzing fear, sexual repression, and, finally, retreat. . . .

The Feminist Philosophy of Domestic Violence

The feminist view of domestic violence . . . is akin to the feminist view of rape—namely, that all men are potential batterers and that battery is an expression of patriarchal control. In a dozen states, including Massachusetts, Colorado, Florida, Washington and Texas (with a dozen more coming down the pike), state guidelines for handling domestic-abuse cases specifically forbid couples' counseling until and unless the man has undergone feminist indoctrination first.

The man is seen by feminists as the problem in *all* domestic-violence situations. It is natural, if you already know who's at fault, to leave the woman out of counseling. To include her would amount to blaming the victim.

Mona Charen, *Conservative Chronicle*, August 20, 1997.

Current feminists say they are trying to help rape victims. But are they? If the women's movement wants to reduce the occurrence of rape, it would put pressure on law-enforcement agencies to catch, convict, incarcerate, and, if possible, treat rapists. If our country spent a fraction of the time and money on fighting rape that has gone into fighting drugs, immense changes would occur. If current feminists were interested in enhancing public sympathy for the victims of sexual assault, they would show it as it is: brutal, ugly, vicious, and traumatic. They would not trivialize rape by lumping it together with consensual sex or unwanted grandfatherly hugs. "If you start calling anything rape, then it takes away from the real rape where you are walking down the street and you are completely physically overtaken and there is nothing you can do about it," Esther Pettibone, a twenty-five-year-old welder from the state of Washington, comments with regard to rape redefinitions. "Then you'll tell someone you got raped and it'll be like, oh well, she got her butt touched. Big deal."

Today's feminists are using the word *rape*—and the fear it invokes—to promote their agenda of victim mythology. It is a method used by many advocacy groups. Anti-abortionists parade photos of bloody fetuses in an effort to outlaw abortion even in the case of rape and incest. Anyone disagreeing is decried with shouts of "babykillers." Current feminists use the word *rape* to push the Victorian vision of women as helpless victims and then label anyone who questions this repressive view "antifeminist."

It is an effective method for pushing victim mythology, but it doesn't help rape victims. In fact, it does them great harm. Their experiences, lost in numbers that include consensual sex, are trivialized.

"[Bodily] insecurity has been instilled into women over generations; we have made not the least headway in the struggle to dispel it."

Women Are Harmed by Societal Standards of Beauty

Germaine Greer

Feminist activist Germaine Greer argues in the subsequent viewpoint that society expects women to meet unrealistic standards of beauty. The pressure women face to look eternally young, beautiful, and thin makes them abnormally preoccupied with their appearance and induces them to spend large amounts of money on useless products. Greer is the author of a variety of books on feminism, including *The Whole Woman*, from which this viewpoint is excerpted.

As you read, consider the following questions:

1. How does society impel women to buy useless beauty products, as claimed by Greer?
2. According to the author, how do most women feel about their appearance?
3. As stated by the author, what does consumer research report about anti-aging products?

Every woman knows that, regardless of all her other achievements, she is a failure if she is not beautiful. She also knows that whatever beauty she has is leaving her, stealthily, day by day.

Even if she is as freakishly beautiful as the supermodels whose images she sees replicated all around her until they are more familiar than the features of her own mother, she cannot be beautiful enough. There must be bits of her that will not do: her knees, her feet, her buttocks, her breasts.

However much body hair she has, it is too much. However little and sweetly she sweats, it is too much. Left to her own devices, she is sure to smell bad. If her body is thin enough, her breasts are sad. If her breasts are full, her arse is surely too big.

What is pathological behaviour in a man is required of a woman. A bald man who wears a wig is a ridiculous figure; a bald woman who refuses to wear a wig is being stroppy and confrontational. Women with "too much" (i.e., any) body hair are expected to struggle daily with depilatories of all kinds in order to appear hairless.

Body Dysmorphic Disorder

Scientists call abnormal preoccupation with a perceived defect in one's appearance Body Dysmorphic Disorder, or BDD. Yet no one would say that the woman who puts herself through the agonising ordeal of hot-waxing her bikini-line must be suffering from BDD.

Such insecurity has been instilled into women over generations; we have made not the least headway in the struggle to dispel it. Every issue of every woman's magazine exploits women's anxiety about "unwanted hair."

Even if you escape hairiness, you will fall foul of cellulite. When *The Female Eunuch* was written, "cellulite" was a French disease. The English word should by rights be "cellulitis," but, as British pharmaceutical companies jumped on a bandwagon set off by sales campaigns for French products, they adopted the French word.

Cellulite is subcutaneous fat, pure and simple. It keeps women warm and softens the contours of their bodies and, if it builds up, it often dimples. Whether or not your fat dimples is a matter of genetic endowment; some women have tight smooth fat and some women have softer fat, which droops and dimples, even on their knees, invariably on their bottoms.

The characteristic orange-peel appearance can be seen even in the bottoms of babies who have not eaten chocolate, drunk coffee or alcohol or smoked, or committed any other of the sins that are punishable by cellulite.

Once upon a time, men and women both admired dimply fat; it took 20th-century marketing to render it disgusting. Most of what is written about "globular fat cells," "poor lymphatic drainage" and "toxins that have solidified" is cynical tosh.

Dimply fat will only disappear if it is starved off; no amount of pounding or vibrating or massaging will have any effect on it whatsoever. No cream, whether made of placenta or the brains of aborted fetuses or ground glass, will break down cellulite. Your cellulite is you, and will be with you till death or liposuction, which is expensive and extremely painful and sometimes more disfiguring than the dimply fat itself.

As fat distribution is hormonally regulated, the fat will probably build up again gradually after liposuction. As cellulite will neither kill you nor go away, it is a goldmine for doctors, nutritionists, naturopaths, aromatherapists, fitness experts and lifestyle managers.

The manufacturers of creams, exercise equipment, skin brushes and dietary supplements all make a bundle out of women's carefully cultivated disgust with their own bodies, scarfed about as they are by "unsightly fat cells." Criminalising cellulite is just another way of demonising fat, any fat, anywhere.

Inducing Women to Buy Useless Products

As a way of inducing them to buy products of no use or value, women have been deliberately infected with BDD. Conditions that practically all women "suffer from" are spoken of as unsightly and abnormal, to make women feel that parts of their bodies, perhaps their whole bodies, are defective and should be worked on, even surgically altered.

Most women think that their hair is not good enough and dye it or bleach it or perm it. Most women feel that their legs are not long enough, that their thighs are too heavy or not firm enough. Most women are unhappy about their bottoms, which are either too flat, too low-slung, too fat or too broad. Preoccupation about her appearance goes some way towards ruining some part of every women's day. Multi-million-dollar industries exploit both her need for reassurance and her need to do something about the way she looks.

The Objectification of Women and Girls

When it comes to growing up in our Barbie Doll culture, girls have an uphill battle. They come of age in a crucible of judging eyes—others' and their own—giving rise to bulimia, anorexia and layers of make-up and confusion. . . . Women and girls are routinely objectified in ways that their male counterparts simply are not, forced to negotiate hostile terrain literally at every turn. . . .

When I consider what comprises the domain of choices we offer girls, I see a profusion of spurious and beguiling claptrap and a dearth of genuine role models. Too often, those who are remain subject to evaluation—sometimes unspoken, other times quite public—based on their looks. Whether it's the First Lady's hairdos and fat ankles or the good-looking kindergarten teacher, from professional conferences to street corners, it's the same story: Looks get you noticed, whether you want to be or not. Female role models are habitually reduced to their physical appearance.

Thomas J. McCarthy, *America*, October 16, 1999.

Thirty years ago, it was enough to look beautiful; now a woman has to have a tight, toned body, including her buttocks and thighs, so that she is good to touch, all over. "Remember," she will be told, "beauty starts from within," so she keeps her bowels open with plenty of fibre and her kidneys flushed with lots of pure water.

Being beautiful from within takes even more time than slapping beauty on from without. Demi Moore is said to work out for four hours a day, beginning with a cardiovascular aerobic workout, then working her legs and buttocks with pliés, standing lunges and thigh lifts, her upper body with shoulder and punching exercises, and toning her abdominal muscles. She also eats only non-processed, pesticide-free, totally vegetarian foods.

The result—taut abs, a rock-hard butt and twanging musculature—was still not enough to save her marriage.

Whatever a woman does, she must not look her age. The fitness regime is lifelong, to go with the lifelong sexual activity that is nowadays obligatory.

Teaching Little Girls to Use Make-Up

The UK beauty industry takes £8–9 billion a year out of women's pockets. Magazines financed by the beauty industry teach little girls that they need make-up and train them to use it, so establishing their lifelong reliance on beauty products.

Not content with showing pre-teens how to use foundations, powders, concealers, blushers, eye-shadows, eye-liners, lip-liners, lipstick and lip gloss, the magazines identify problems of dryness, flakiness, blackheads, shininess, dullness, blemishes, puffiness, oiliness, spots, greasiness, that little girls are meant to treat with moisturisers, fresheners, masks, packs, washes, lotions, cleansers, toners, scrubs, astringents—none of which will make the slightest difference and all of which would cost money the child does not have.

Pre-teen cosmetics are relatively cheap but, within a few years, more sophisticated marketing will have persuaded the most level-headed young woman to throw money away on alchemical preparations containing anything from silk to cashmere, pearls, proteins, royal jelly, placenta extracts, ceramides, biotin, collagen, "phytotensers," bisabolol, jojoba, "hydra-captors," serine, fruit hydroxy-acids, oleospheres, corneospheres, nanovectors, glycerol—anything real or phony that might fend off her imminent collapse into hideous decrepitude.

Yet consumer research regularly reports that nothing applied to the surface of the skin can affect the underlying structures or prevent aging, and still the anti-aging products sell.

Every day, hospitals put placenta into special freezers to be collected once a week by unmarked vans and sold to face-cream manufacturers. So desperate are some women to stave off aging that they are prepared to submit to injections of botulin toxin to freeze their facial muscles and prevent wrinkles.

A Global Pandemic

What is truly depressing about the false dawn of feminism is that, as we have been congratulating ourselves on largely imaginary victories, BDD has become a global pandemic. Women who were unselfconscious and unmade-up 30 years ago, who walked at a natural pace and worked alongside men in the fields and the factories, are now infected.

In provincial cities in China, hanging up over shop doorways, you can see boards with padded brassieres pinned all over them, and trays of cheap lacquer and lipstick under flyspotted glass, so that women who are naturally small-breasted can assume the "new shape." Beauty salons crimp and curl shining hair with a fall like silk into shapeless frizz.

The two billion people worldwide who regularly view "Baywatch" are all recognising a single, tawdry, synthetic kind of skinnied-down, pumped-up, bleached and depilated female beauty. Real girls tell me that when they run along the beach, their male companions make fun of their real breasts that bounce up and down—unlike the rigid half-tennis-ball boobs of the "Baywatch" babes.

Who cares that Pamela Anderson, who has been put together out of all the movable parts of male and female fetishism, has been abused by her husband? We are selling fantasy here.

| "There seems to be a far greater understanding among women today that they no longer have to adhere to a well-prescribed regimen to be considered . . . beautiful."

Women Are Not Harmed by Societal Standards of Beauty

Karen Lehrman

Feminist arguments that societal beauty standards harm women are misguided, contends Karen Lehrman in the subsequent viewpoint. In fact, she maintains, standards of female beauty have relaxed considerably in recent years; while some women elect to follow the dictates of the fashion industry, many do not. Moreover, she writes, society's beauty standards have helped women by emphasizing the importance of exercise and healthy eating. Lehrman is the author of *The Lipstick Proviso: Women, Sex, and Power in the Real World*, from which this viewpoint is excerpted.

As you read, consider the following questions:
1. What examples does Lehrman give to show that contemporary society no longer promotes rigid standards of female beauty?
2. What is the feminist critique of beauty, as explained by the author?
3. According to the author, what should be the ultimate feminist goal, with regard to beauty?

In recent years, thanks largely to the feminist critique, notions of beauty have begun to expand beyond the Barbie standard. A few decades ago you'd have been hard-pressed to find even a brunette on the cover of a fashion magazine. Today, advertisers and editors will fairly regularly use not just brunettes, but women who are black, Hispanic, and Asian; even women over forty (Lauren Hutton, Isabella Rossellini) are now frequently interspersed among the nymphets. You can also find a far wider range of types, both facial (a somewhat crooked nose, eyes close together) and body (from gamine waifs to muscular jocks to curvaceous sirens). Several of the top models, especially Kristen McMenamy, are distinctive far more for their quirky features and attitude than for their beauty.

More important, there seems to be a far greater understanding among women today that they no longer have to adhere to a well-prescribed regimen to be considered womanly, or even beautiful. Women follow certain beauty rites and rituals but not others—and each woman chooses differently. Some women refuse to shave their legs and underarms but have no problem wearing lipstick and mascara and having their hair permed. Others refrain from makeup and jewelry but have their noses "fixed" and unwanted hair removed. Women today are also far less likely to change their entire wardrobes to accommodate the latest fashion.

The Feminist Critique of Beauty

Despite such apparent progress, in recent years the reigning feminist critique of beauty has taken on a "political" slant. The beauty ideal, claim many feminists, is not merely a cultural fixation with destructive side effects. Rather, it is a patriarchal ploy used both to control women morally and sexually and to earn profits for the "male-dominated" medical, cosmetic, diet, and fashion industries. The more progress women make, the argument now goes, the more society has forced women to abide by an increasingly strict and restrictive beauty ideal.

In *The Beauty Myth*, Naomi Wolf argues that the recent rise in cases of anorexia is due to society's "material vested interest in [women's] troubles with eating. . . . Dieting is the most potent political sedative in women's history; a quietly mad population is a tractable one." In *Backlash*, Susan Faludi claims that misogynist fashion designers began pushing seductive clothes during the eighties (corsets, miniskirts, lingerie) to impede women's progress, attempting to reduce women to the status of passive sex objects. These feminists and others cite the recent increase in sales of beauty products and services as proof that the backlash has been successful.

Some theorists take this argument yet another step, arguing that not only is a specific ideal of beauty constructed by society, but so is the very notion of beauty itself. According to Wolf and others, there is no quality called "beauty" that objectively and universally exists. Various academic feminists argue that the entire field of aesthetics is an instrument of "bourgeois hegemony."

To disempower "beauty" once and for all, many of these feminist theorists argue, the "fashion-beauty complex" of advertising, women's magazines, and the fashion and cosmetic industries must be dismantled. The media must only use "real" women of all shapes, sizes, and colors, and Hollywood must end its love affair with pretty women. Only then will women be able to accept themselves the way they are and devote their time and energy to far more important matters.

Beauty Is Not a Myth

If only it were that simple. Fortunately, beauty is not a myth, an arbitrary cultural convention, an ideological fabrication. Beauty is a reality, a gift of God, nature, or genius that, to some extent, transcends culture and history. Society has certainly exploited a female obsession with youth and beauty, but society, ours or anyone else's, didn't create it. The real culprit is evolution: while men have historically competed for women through bravery and brawn, women have competed for men through displays of reproductive fitness. Different cultures and eras have emphasized different features and body types, but physical female beauty has been a relatively stable commodity, and women's desire to attain it is buried deep within their psyches.

It is true that many women still destroy their bodies in the name of beauty—smoking, starving, or vomiting to lose weight; basking in the deadly sun; wearing toe-curling spikes; ingesting the latest miracle potion promising eternal youth. And according to at least one study, the number of women who view their bodies in a less than loving way has more than doubled in the past twenty years—nearly half of all women (compared with a third of men) say they are dissatisfied with their bodies. Yet the explanations seem to be far more complicated than the backlash analysis would suggest. In fact, feminism itself may be partly responsible for the rise in eating disorders.

Beauty Standards Come from Women, Not Society or Men

Two [*Journal of Abnormal Psychology*] researchers . . . looked at the preferences for women's body size in both men and women. Subjects were presented with nine female figures, ranging from very thin to very plump.

Both men and women were asked what body size they prefer. Women were also asked to identify the ideal size for themselves, and what they perceived men's ideal female figure was. In both cases, women selected a figure slimmer than average, but men selected a figure of average body size.

The most immediate conclusion from this study is that women erroneously believe that men desire women who are emaciated. In fact, men are more forgiving of women's body size than women are.

The broader implication, which the authors don't address, is that the main social pressure for women's body size comes, not from the media or men, but from women themselves. Women most likely perpetuate this beauty standard through conversations with other women, focusing on their own dissatisfaction with their body size, or their efforts to become slimmer. Another, less noble source, probably comes from disparaging comments about other women's weight. This behaviour suggests that women are concerned about their beauty, not to compete for men, but to compete against other women.

Chester V. Farely, *Forum*, February 21, 1997.

At the same time, feminism has surely allowed women to broaden the venues for gaining self-respect, and has begun to break society's nasty habit of equating a woman's worth with her beauty. A woman sitting on the Supreme Court or on a corporate board doesn't have to be beautiful to command respect; drop-dead looks might even undermine her ability to be taken seriously.

Aesthetics and Autonomy Can Coexist

What feminism can't do much about is society's general appreciation of beautiful women. Nor should it. Aesthetics and autonomy can happily coexist. Insisting that cosmetics and fashion are tools of the patriarchy leaves women with two options: they can either refrain from all traditionally feminine pursuits, and thereby make themselves beauty martyrs; or they can engage in them, and thereby be left with the view that they are victims of male oppression. Yet a woman can reconstruct her face, take two aerobics classes a day, and wear corsets, bustiers, and fishnet stockings, and still be a feminist.

Feminist theorists are hardly the first, of course, to denounce beauty in the name of a higher good. The Puritans believed that ornament and sensuality distracted women (and men) from their spiritual duties. A drab proletarian chic was practically an article of faith among the fellow-traveling set during communism's heyday and was picked up again, with variations, by privileged revolutionary students of the sixties.

Damning Beauty Is Counterproductive

Not only is damning beauty unnecessary to a feminist revolution then. It is also counterproductive. Much of what is touted as promoting beauty today—exercising vigorously, eating nutritionally, ingesting or applying various herbs and vitamins—is also good for one's health: the ironic truth is that many women don't focus as much as they should on their bodies. Blame and self-pity may feel comforting, but many of the problems our bodies encounter are our own fault. And it's not a coincidence that women who feel good about themselves physically tend to feel good about themselves emotionally. It's also not a coincidence that when women treat themselves well, they are not apt to allow others to treat them poorly.

There's also much women can do themselves to change their relationship with beauty. The fact that beauty is a reality makes it no less of a tyranny. Indeed, it makes it more so: some things will never change, no matter how much women achieve. Yet women can, for one, toughen themselves emotionally, so that they can withstand potentially hurtful remarks or societal messages. Hyperanalyzing fashion, advertisements, and sexual imagery, on the other hand, really doesn't help women very much on a daily basis. It also encourages a society-is-destiny view: women's lives won't change until society does.

Perhaps the ultimate feminist goal is to move beyond the injustice of beauty, to be able to appreciate its magnificence while ignoring its perversions, to be able to look at a beautiful woman with awe and only a tinge of resentment. That's hard work. Indeed, allowing beautiful women their beauty may turn out to be one of the more difficult aspects of personal liberation.

Periodical Bibliography

The following articles have been selected to supplement the diverse views presented in this chapter. Addresses are provided for periodicals not indexed in the *Readers' Guide to Periodical Literature*, the *Alternative Press Index*, the *Social Sciences Index*, or the *Index to Legal Periodicals and Books*.

Natalie Zemon Davis and Jill Ker Conway	"The Rest of the Story," *New York Times Magazine*, May 16, 1999.
The Economist	"A Century of Struggle, Progress for Women," *San Diego Union-Tribune*, December 5, 1999.
Suzanne Fields	"When Women Mind Their Own Business," *Insight*, June 29, 1998. Available at 3600 New York Ave. NE, Washington, DC 20002.
Evan Gahr	"Uncovering the Politics of Women's Magazines," *Wall Street Journal*, August 21, 1997.
Steven Hill and Rob Richie	"American Women Have a Long Way to Go," *Progressive Populist*, February 15, 2000. Available from PO Box 150517, Austin, TX 78715-0517.
Molly Ivins	"A Salute to the Founding Mothers," *Liberal Opinion*, March 22, 1999. Available from PO Box 880, Vinton, IA 52349-0880.
Barbara Dafoe Whitehead	"The Girls of Gen X," *American Enterprise*, January/February 1998.

CHAPTER 2

How Has Feminism Affected Society?

Chapter Preface

Generally, both feminists and those who are critical of feminism agree that the women's movement benefited women by expanding their opportunities within the workplace. However, with regard to feminism's overall effect on society, these two groups possess strong ideological differences, principally over the issue of marriage.

Elizabeth Fox-Genovese, author of the book Feminism Is Not the Story of My Life: *How Today's Feminist Elite Has Lost Touch with the Real Concerns of Women*, contends that feminists, because they regard husbands and children as unfair burdens on women, have engaged in a campaign "to secure women's complete freedom from marriage, including the freedom to leave a marriage at will, never to marry, and to bear children outside marriage without sacrifice of respectability." According to Fox-Genovese, feminist attacks on marriage harm children, who benefit from a traditional, two-parent family, as well as women themselves, who want the emotional intimacy and economic security of marriage.

In response to these criticisms, many feminists argue that feminism does not oppose—and in fact supports—marriage. As editor Frances Coleman writes, "Feminism wasn't, and isn't about destroying families or obliterating traditional roles. It's about choices: to become a mother, or not; to stay at home with the children, or work outside the home; to have an undemanding job or climb the career ladder." Other feminists maintain that feminism is justified in criticizing marriage. Arguing that the traditional nuclear family relies on the submissiveness of women, writer Urvashi Vaid states that "the old nuclear, patriarchal family does not work; it is permeated with violence, drug and alcohol abuse, and unhappiness. [Feminists] need to vigorously defend single, two-parent, and extended families whose values are love and commitment, not the subjugation of women."

The debate over how feminists regard marriage—and whether or not feminists should criticize marriage—is examined in the following chapter. In this chapter, authors provide disparate views on the effects of feminism on women and society.

"Few [American] girls grow up without the widest sense of personal options in the world."

Feminism Has Expanded Women's Choices

Elinor Burkett

Elinor Burkett, author of *The Right Women: A Journey Through the Heart of Conservative America*, from which the subsequent viewpoint was excerpted, contends that feminism has dramatically expanded women's choices and opportunities. As a direct result of the feminist movement, Burkett writes, large numbers of women are obtaining advanced degrees, working as high-powered executives, heading their own businesses, and serving in public office. Moreover, feminists have succeeded in dismantling laws that once prevented women from obtaining credit, divorce, control over their own bodies, and equal access to jobs and housing.

As you read, consider the following questions:

1. According to Burkett, how did the feminists of the 1960s envision the future?
2. What evidence does the author provide that feminism has improved women's lives?
3. As cited by the author, what widely accepted tenets of feminism were once considered to be "revolutionary doctrines"?

My mother, Anna, was the woman Betty Friedan had in mind when she wrote *The Feminine Mystique* in 1963. One of the first female graduates of the University of Pennsylvania, Anna was bright, curious and bored out of her mind staying home to raise her two daughters. She kept herself busy helping my father in his business and working with various civic groups, but I always wondered why she hadn't followed her early dream and gone to medical school. She refused to satisfy my curiosity. "I guess it just wasn't important enough to me," she responded dismissively whenever I broached the topic. My father was equally unhelpful. All he could say was that my mother had never brought up the idea in the years after the depression, when they could have afforded the luxury.

The question hung over our household as my sister and I grew up, and it was resolved, in an odd way, when we came of age, and headed for the type of career my mother had forsaken. I thought I was following the advice my father had given me explicitly: Don't worry about getting married and having children. Go to school. Find a career. Make something of yourself. Only years later did I understand that I was also following the advice my mother had given me less overtly: Don't end up like me.

What About Women?

Entering college in 1964, I joined a wave of other women who had also tasted their mothers' frustration and forged it into a weapon against a nation that had forgotten its own women. Simply by asking the question "What about women?" we reimagined America and stormed Washington, Bismarck, Sacramento and every possible political center with scores of demands, from equal wages to safe streets. We created a new language and wove it into the lives of the next generation. We rewrote the nation's understanding of its past in the hope of reshaping its future.

The shape of that future seemed absolutely, glaringly clear to us: Women would discover their potential, throw off the shackles of outmoded roles and oppressive stereotypes and take their rightful places in politics, science, business and the arts. Men might balk and struggle to retain their supremacy, but in the end, they would either grow to appreciate the rich-

Women in the United States Congress

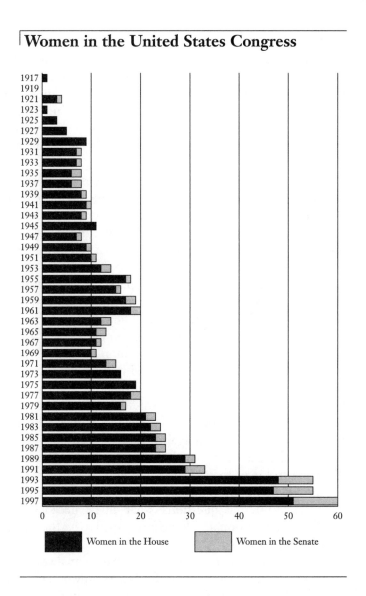

| | Women in the House | Women in the Senate |

ness of equality or be vanquished by the power of national sisterhood. Young women and their brothers would grow up in a world in which Johnnie would feel free to dance to Stravinsky and Susi could gravitate toward welding. And with women in a position of full equality, women's nature—women's sensitivity and intuitiveness—would make America a kinder and gentler place. . . .

New Opportunities for Women

Three decades after Betty Friedan touched a national nerve with *The Feminine Mystique*, girls are no longer consigned to home economics while boys trudge to woodworking and shop. No newspaper would dare divide its Help Wanted section into male and female categories. No university would refuse to promote a faculty member simply because she was a woman.

Today more bachelor's and master's degrees are awarded to women than to men. In 1996, women made up more than half the freshman class at Yale Medical School and 45 percent of the graduating class of its law school. In the past ten years alone, the number of female executive vice presidents of businesses has more than doubled, while the number of female senior vice presidents rose 75 percent. Women now own 40 percent of all retail and service businesses, employing a staggering 15.5 million people. The year Friedan published her seminal work, only fourteen women served in the United States Congress; by 1996, the number had risen to fifty-six, and female candidates are winning their races for political office at the same rate as their male counterparts.

Violence against women has hardly disappeared, but it is no longer the sort of taboo which made the women who appeared at the first speak-out against rape in New York feminist heroines. Dozens of laws that kept women from credit, divorce, control over their own bodies and choices in housing or employment have vanished into the dustbin of history. And virtually no one questions what three decades ago seemed like revolutionary doctrines: equal pay for equal work and equal access to jobs.

While no rational person could claim that a female nirvana has been created in Peoria or Seattle, American women think differently about their lives now than they did in the 1950s, and so do American men. Few girls grow up without the widest sense of personal options in the world. Few grown women don't know that they have the right to get angry, get a job, or get divorced. Measured against three millennia of women's history, the progress has been breathtaking.

*"Many . . . modern women complain . . .
that they don't have the 'choices' their own
mothers had."*

Feminism Has Limited Women's Choices

Danielle Crittenden

In the following viewpoint, Danielle Crittenden argues that
while feminism may have expanded women's opportunities
in the workplace, it has stifled women's personal lives by encouraging women to pursue careers at the expense of marriage and children. In their effort to prove that women could
be fully independent, feminists have neglected the fact that
most women consider family to be the most important aspect of their lives. Crittenden is the author of *What Our
Mothers Didn't Tell Us: Why Happiness Eludes the Modern
Woman.* She is the former editor of the *Women's Quarterly,* a
publication of the Independent Women's Forum, a nonprofit organization that promotes individual responsibility,
strong families, and limited government.

As you read, consider the following questions:
1. What is the new "problem with no name," according to
   Crittenden?
2. In the author's opinion, what sort of life would make
   most women happy?
3. As stated by the author, what feminist wisdom did many
   women receive growing up?

Reprinted from "Back to the Future," by Danielle Crittenden, *Women's Quarterly,*
Winter 1999. Reprinted by permission of Danielle Crittenden, author of *What
Our Mothers Didn't Tell Us: Why Happiness Eludes the Modern Woman.*

As editor of this little journal [*The Women's Quarterly*] and a critic of feminism, I've often been accused of wanting to send women "back." Back to where is not usually spelled out. It's supposed to be obvious—back to split-levels and aprons, beehive hairdos and marriages to Ozzie Nelson. To question the impact of the past thirty years of social change upon women's lives is considered a provocative thing to do—at least if you're doing it from a non-feminist point of view. It's sort of like offering to make your husband a martini and fetch his slippers when he gets home from work. Or saying, "Actually I'd rather be at home with my kids than data processing." The first step on the slippery slope back to Fifties Hell.

Feminism's Beliefs and Assumptions

Although feminism, as a conscious political movement, can boast fewer adherents today than the Czech communist party, its beliefs and assumptions about the way women should live their lives remain strong: We have absorbed the lesson that we should forgo—or postpone—marriage and children in order to forge careers; when married, we should not depend upon our husbands, either to stay married to us for the long haul or to support us when we have children; we should not ultimately look to our families for satisfaction or happiness—those things are best realized in our jobs, and in our spiritual growth as individuals.

That this wisdom may be faulty is bitter medicine to have to swallow. So many of us imbibed these ideas and plotted our lives according to them that even as we're reeling from their effect, grasping around for an antidote, we don't want to reject them. Yet reject them we must if we're to begin to solve the problems women face today.

For when you look around at modern women's lives, I think few of us would be able to say confidently that the progress we've made has resulted in net gain. Yes, we are freer than any generation of women in history to hold positions of power in the workplace and in government; but this has come at the expense of power over our personal lives. I've heard many accomplished modern women complain—without irony—that they don't have the "choices" their own mothers had.

Some are college graduates who simply can't figure out how they're going to do it all—or even just one piece of it: find a decent man to marry, have children and a career, and yet also enjoy the sort of family life that was often absent in their own upbringing, as the products of divorced and/or working parents. Some are successful thirtyish vice-presidents of companies or partners in law firms who fret that they will never be able to meet a man or have children. Some are working mothers who feel they have no choice but to work, even while their children are infants—just as a previous generation of women felt they had no choice but to stay home with their kids rather than work.

All of these women are bound together by the same problem: call it a new "problem with no name." And it's exactly the reverse of the old, 1950s problem with no name that Betty Friedan wrote about in her landmark book, *The Feminine Mystique*. In Friedan's time, the problem was that too many people failed to see that while women were women, they were also human, and they were being denied the ability to express and fulfill their potential outside the home. Today the problem is that while we recognize that women are human, we have blinded ourselves to the fact that we are also women. If we feel stunted and oppressed when denied the chance to realize our human potential, we suffer every bit as much when cut off from those aspects of life that are distinctly female—whether it's being a wife or raising children or making a home.

For if, as women, we were all to sit down and honestly attempt to figure out what sort of lives would make us happy, I suspect—assuming the basics like food and adequate income, and leaving aside fantasies of riches and celebrity—that most of our answers would be very similar to one another's, and quite different from men's. They would go something like this: We want to marry husbands who will love and respect and stay with us; we want children; we want to be good mothers. At the same time, many of us will want to pursue interests outside of our families, interests that will vary from woman to woman, depending upon her ambition and talent. Some women will be content with work or involvements that can be squeezed in around their commitments at home; some women will want or need to work at a job, either full- or part-time. Other women may be more ambitious—they may want to be surgeons or executives, politicians or artists. For them the competing demands of family and work will always be difficult to resolve. But I think when we compare our conditions

Women Never Wanted New Roles

Betty Friedan published *The Feminine Mystique* in 1963. It was a transitional document that changed the way women—and therefore men—would see their social roles. A rereading of that book, which became such a Bible for the first wave of modern feminism, shows that the frustrated suburban housewives Friedan interviewed never said they wanted the life stresses of men. They only said they were bored and wanted something more for themselves. Most of these women enjoyed a good family life, but as their children were getting older, the gratifications of being mom were increasingly reduced to chauffeuring and "schlepping" the kids to school, Little League, piano lessons, and the orthodontist. The absence of public transportation in the suburbs was crucial to this phenomenon.

These suburban women were not hostile toward men, nor did they want to reject the dominant roles they maintained in family life. If Friedan had asked the women she interviewed whether they would have preferred working in high-powered (i.e., stressful) jobs when their children were young, I think they would have been shocked and turned off by the idea. They wanted to be more creative, which meant working to earn money in part-time jobs, or to go back to college to train for something in the future when their children were grown and gone. But I suspect none of them wanted an absolute 50-50 relationship of work (i.e., earning power) instead of being the mom. . . .

By 1981, when *The Second Stage* was published, Friedan was hearing a different complaint. She was in California in the office of a television producer who pulled her aside to talk to her privately. This woman, in her late 20s, was not only "dressed for success," but she looked like the fulfillment of the feminist crusade: an executive with power and a good paycheck. "I know I'm lucky to have this job," she told Friedan, "but you people who fought for these things had your families. You already had your men and children. What are we supposed to do?"

Suzanne Fields, *Heritage Lectures*, March 26, 1997.

for happiness, most of our lists would share these essentials. The women who don't desire these things—those who like living alone or who find perfectly fulfilling the companionship of their friends and cats or whose work eclipses their need for family—may be sincerely happy, but they should not be confused with the average woman.

Women's Preferences for Marriage, Children, and Career

The Roper Starch polling firm has asked American women every few years since 1974 about their preferences for marriage, children and career. The poll conducted in 1995 shows that the majority of women—55 percent—hope to combine all three, and a full quarter—26 percent—want marriage and children but not a career.

Unfortunately, for nearly thirty years, the public policies and individual ways of life that feminists have encouraged, and the laws they have pushed through, have been based on their adamant belief that women want more than equality with men or options outside their families; they want full independence from husbands and families.

And this is where ground zero of the debate is today. It's not about "going back"—as if that were even possible! Nor is it about whether women should have to make the Sophie's Choice decision of work versus children. It's about the best way to realize our aspirations—all of them. In order to do that, we have to begin by rejecting the ingrained feminist assumption that for most of us our happiness is something that can be achieved independently of men and family.

The feminist wisdom so many of us received growing up—to delay marriage, to delay children, to put everything into our work—may help us achieve good jobs, but little else. It's harder to meet and attract men in your thirties than in your twenties; it's more difficult to start families later in life, not to mention extremely inconvenient to have to deal with a newborn in mid-career. It's also very tough, in the aftermath of the sexual revolution, to find men willing to marry and take on the responsibilities of family when there's a big supply of single women out there willing to sleep with them without demanding commitment in return.

In my new book, *What Our Mothers Didn't Tell Us: Why Happiness Eludes the Modern Woman*, I propose that we do go back at least in one sense—to the idea of early marriage, and motherhood. Contrary to feminist wisdom, if a woman today marries in her early twenties and has children soon after, she is not condemning herself (if that is the word) to a life of domesticity like her grandmother. She is instead settling her personal life early, when it is easiest to do it, and freeing herself up for a career (if that's what she chooses), when her children are older and in school. And if enough of us are willing to do this, we also shut down the system of no-strings-attached sex that has so benefited men and injured women.

Feminists will of course reject this idea, but that's because they insist on taking an androgynous view of the sexes, in which the only way we can maintain women's equality is if we do precisely the same things and occupy precisely the same roles in life as men, whether it's changing diapers and taking out the garbage or fighting fires and going into combat. The moment a woman admits to wanting to be a wife, or to care for her children, she is seen as somehow letting down the side. But these desires persist, intensely. Perhaps that's why feminists have supported Bill Clinton so vehemently: Like him they believe that if a fact is denied, it ceases to exist.

But as so many of my generation have found, while independence might be nice as a young single woman, it's not so nice as a single mother or as a single forty-year-old. And if we want to change our situation, we may not need to *go* back but we may have to begin *looking* back, honestly, at some of the ideas we rejected in favor of the often hollow freedom we enjoy today.

"The only result feminists accomplished by endorsing the sexual revolution was to deprive women of the societal support they needed to refuse to engage in casual sex."

The Sexual Revolution Has Harmed Women

F. Carolyn Graglia

The sexual revolution, a movement endorsed by many feminists in the 1960s, encouraged women to reject the double standard that tolerated male promiscuity while expecting women to be sexually reticent. F. Carolyn Graglia asserts in the subsequent viewpoint that the sexual revolution has had a harmful effect on women. Prior to the sexual revolution, she claims, women controlled the sexual aspects of their relationships with men; most women chose to forgo premarital sex, at least until marriage was imminent. Graglia contends that the sexual revolution, by making casual sex the norm, deprived women of the societal support they needed to refuse sex. In addition, she writes, the sexual revolution exacerbated tensions between the sexes by making men feel as though they were being judged on their sexual performance. Graglia is the author of *Domestic Tranquility: A Brief Against Feminism*.

As you read, consider the following questions:
1. Why did women in the 1940s and 1950s shun promiscuity, according to Graglia?
2. In the author's view, how do men and women differ in their taste for premarital sexual activity?
3. What traits do men value in a spouse, as reported by Graglia?

Excerpted from *Domestic Tranquility*, by F. Carolyn Graglia. Copyright ©1997 by F. Carolyn Graglia. Reprinted by permission of Spence Publishing Company.

By endorsing the sexual revolution, feminists persuaded many women to adopt male patterns of sexual behavior. They encouraged women to reject the double standard that tolerated male promiscuity while expecting the female to cultivate modesty, sexual reticence, and discretion. They regarded this double standard as one of the worst abuses of patriarchal oppression of women. Instead, by abandoning this double standard, women lost their sexual power.

Even critics of other aspects of feminist ideology subscribe to the myth that the double standard was an affliction to women. A typical example is writer Katherine Kersten's belief that "women have benefited significantly from their newfound sexual autonomy" afforded by the sexual revolution.

But to credit the sexual revolution with giving us previously unavailable sexual opportunities is to believe that there has ever been a time in history when relationships were marred by the man's refusal to have sex with a willing woman. The only result feminists accomplished by endorsing the sexual revolution was to deprive women of the societal support they needed to refuse to engage in casual sex. Women in my generation, growing up in the 1940s and 1950s, did not lack opportunities to engage in premarital sex. We could grow up without being remotely sequestered (lying about my age, I obtained my first job at fourteen, working a night shift with working-class men). We could enjoy the best education. We could have a profession that guaranteed us complete financial independence. But some of us shunned promiscuity nonetheless.

That's because we would have felt demeaned and degraded by the casual sexual activities that were being urged upon us by feminist sexual revolutionaries and artfully justified as harmless sources of pleasure by men like Judge Richard A. Posner. In *Sex and Reason*, this erudite economist and jurist tells us that the "traditional female role, in which premarital virginity and marital chastity are so emphasized, is an impediment to women's educational and occupational, as well as their sexual, equality."

Posner offers no other coherent reason for condemning the sexual modesty and reticence integral to traditional femininity. Why would premarital virginity and marital chastity impede either a woman's educational or occupational endeavors? It was certainly never my experience that they did. They were, on the contrary, part of a sexual ethos which protected me from what could have been distracting and personally harmful interference with my academic and career pursuits.

Women once confidently controlled the sexual aspects of their dating relationships, setting and enforcing the rules while viewing the male as a suppliant who would be grateful for whatever sexual favors he received (which usually would be something short of intercourse). Not yet misled by feminist teachings, females knew these were favors. Cultural mores entitled us to rebuff sexual advances because no one believed male and female sexuality were the same or that women's craving for casual sexual activity equaled men's.

The woman also knew that there was nothing wrong with her feeling this way; to suggest that her equality with males required that she pretend otherwise would have seemed absurd. No one questioned that men and women differed in their taste for premarital sexual activity: The average man, we knew, was born with lust in his heart for raw sex; the average woman, with a yearning for romance, and the ability, if given the right circumstances, to cultivate a taste for satisfying her physical lust through sexual intercourse. Casual sexual activity, we also knew, was ill-suited to providing those circumstances.

Having absorbed feminist teachings, women became confused and diffident as to their right to control the nature and extent of premarital sexual activity. They feared that less-than-enthusiastic participation would establish their difference from, and hence their inequality with, men. Today, well-educated, professional women, who are embarrassed to defend the unsophisticated concepts of virginity and chastity, are less competent to control men's sexual advances than high school girls in the 1940s.

One result is the invention of concepts like "date rape" and an expansive law of sexual harassment in an attempt to provide the protection for women against seduction that unsophisticated high school girls once felt completely confident in securing for themselves with a graceful—and, we sometimes thought, even elegant—refusal. These concepts are simply desperate attempts to distort the criminal law in order to reassert some form of female control over ordinary dating relationships. The feminists' new campaign demonstrates how vulnerably bereft of self-confidence women have become since feminist sexual revolutionaries convinced society that women share a male appetite for promiscuous sex. Feminism has attempted to justify its endorsement of the sexual revolution, however, as a way to acquaint women with sexual fulfillment.

In *Re-Making Love: The Feminization of Sex*, Barbara Ehrenreich, *et al.*, argued that it was because women's sexual satisfaction had not counted before that female sexual revolutionaries became obsessed with the topic of their orgasms. But this is not so. Rather, it was the attempt to imitate stereotypical male sexual activity—sex without the magic and mystery of romance—that resulted in casual sexual relationships in which nothing counted but the orgasm. At the same time, the casualness of these couplings was inconsistent with female orgasmic satisfaction, a more complicated goal than male ejaculation. Women's dissatisfaction with the fruits of loveless sex led to a great demanding by them of men's sexual performance. And from the men's perspective, this demandingness was particularly pernicious because women's increased participation in promiscuous sex invited knowledgeable comparisons of men's sexual performance.

The traditional dating system prevailing before the sexual revolution had always fostered a certain antagonism between men and women. As Christopher Lasch has noted, the system involved a solidarity between members of the same sex combined with an attitude of ridicule toward, and a cynical willingness to exploit, the opposite sex. College students were inclined to "pretend a ruthlessness toward the opposite sex which they did not feel." After playing out this dating ritual, the participants usually found someone who convinced them to abandon the emotional defense of ridicule and acknowledge an incipient love. Throughout the enterprise, wherever she drew the line within the range of sexual possibilities, a woman usually held herself unavailable for sexual intercourse, at least until marriage was imminent. Despite the man's complaints, this unavailability had the benefit of freeing him from the full obligations of sexual performance until a time when he could feel more secure in the woman's affections. At that time, he could still be fairly certain that—whatever his capabilities as a lover—the woman would not have much experience on which to base comparisons.

Casualties of the Sexual Revolution

Women, tasting the bitter aftermath, have taken to blaming men for the sexual revolution, which has turned them into unpaid prostitutes.

But the sexual revolution was not a male thing. It was a feminist-led revolution to liberate women from chastity. . . .

Evidence is accumulating, however, that a woman's nature is different and that promiscuity erodes her capacity for intimacy. Not physical intimacy, of course, but that emotional intimacy that is the true basis of a successful marriage. A woman entices the male with sex. If she has had umpteen partners before she marries, she may not experience the emotional bond from giving herself to her husband.

My conversations with the younger set support this conclusion. Young women tell me that it is hard to find marriage-minded men, and young men tell me that it is hard to propose to whores.

Paul Craig Roberts, *Conservative Chronicle*, August 11, 1999.

The new sexual ethos created by the sexual revolution exacerbated the antagonisms of traditional dating relationships and—as Isaac Bashevis Singer powerfully puts it in his condemnation of this ethos—"transformed sex into a marketplace with competitors." Ehrenreich, *et al.*, acknowledged men's sense of injury, citing critics who characterized as "frightening" this "focus on the female orgasm and performance evaluation" of the male, who believed that men do not want women "to be very sexually experienced," and who speculated that "women's clitoral obsessions were driving men to homosexuality." Midge Decter described the sexual pursuits of college students as causing the girls to feel "themselves manipulated and mistreated by males," and the boys to line up "in droves at the student health services seeking help with a problem" that "once unmasked, is either the fear of, or the actual onset of, impotence."

Sociologist Charles Winick suggested that contemporary men's greater misgivings about their sexual performance may be partly due to women's attitude that their failure to obtain orgasms readily meant they were being cheated by men. Compounding the pressures of coping with sexually aggressive, demanding, and experienced women was the new competition men faced as increasing numbers of women entered the workplace. The toll these pressures took helps explain those effete, attenuated males whose sexual fires, in my husband's description, appear to have banked without ever blazing forth.

Men's predicament reminds me of a Labrador retriever we once had who growled so ferociously whenever someone rang our doorbell that we held her collar to prevent her from lunging at the screen door. Late one night, when two threatening men stood outside the screen door, my husband let go of her collar. Instead of lunging, she stopped growling and looked up at him as if to ask why he was no longer holding her back. The collar of sexual morality, with its expectation of greater sexual reticence on the woman's part, was always slipped by those sufficiently determined to gain release. Many women, however, welcomed the support of this restraint in resisting demands for sexual intercourse, while hoping to retain the man's interest in a dating relationship. For a man, the collar of traditional sexual morality provided welcome validation of his potency through an institutional recognition, as it were, that his rather awesome masculinity required curbing: He was given a reassuring aura of dominance as the potential sexual aggressor, yet unless he chose to, he would usually not be called upon to prove it.

On the basis of his studies of human behavior, psychologist David Buss concludes that American men "view the lack of sexual experience as desirable in a spouse." This is so because men "place a premium on fidelity" and "the single best predictor of extramarital sex is premarital sexual permissiveness." Men rank "faithfulness and sexual loyalty" as a wife's "most highly valued trait" and "abhor promiscuity and infidelity in their wives." When a sexual relationship is threatened, says Buss, women are more likely to feel sad and abandoned, and men to experience rage: "Male sexual jealousy is the single most frequent cause of all types of violence directed at wives," and most spousal homicide is "precipitated by male accusations of adultery or by the woman's leaving or threatening to leave the husband." These facts of life, now documented by evolutionary psychologists, were always part of our cultural knowledge. They are facts that feminist sexual revolutionaries chose to ignore. While they and the women who followed their lead obtained what they viewed as sexual freedom—that is, the freedom to imitate male tomcat behavior—they jeopardized their chances of marrying and, once married, of remaining so.

> *"The feminist movement has weakened the foundational institution of life—the family—by blurring . . . the roles of husband and wife."*

Feminism Has Caused the Breakdown of the Family

Leslie Anne Carbone

Leslie Anne Carbone is a domestic policy analyst at the Family Research Council, a nonprofit, nonpartisan educational organization that exists to reaffirm and promote the traditional family unit and the Judeo-Christian value system upon which it is built. She maintains in the subsequent viewpoint that feminism has weakened the institution of the family by insisting that both women and men abandon their traditional gender roles. Carbone argues that the elimination of these roles has led to the decline of marriage and an increase in divorce and single parenthood—developments that have severe consequences for children and for society as a whole.

As you read, consider the following questions:
1. According to Carbone, what are the different roles fulfilled by husbands and wives?
2. How have feminists challenged the permanence of marriage, in the author's view?
3. What evidence does Carbone provide to support her claim that divorce has severe consequences for children?

The feminist movement has weakened the foundational institution of life—the family—by blurring and blending the roles of husband and wife. Until recent times, most Americans entered marriage with the understanding that husbands and wives fulfilled different roles, each spouse exercising responsibility in different spheres. Reflecting centuries of Western custom and tradition that was informed by Jewish and Christian teaching, the husband was considered the head of the family, responsible to cherish, protect, and provide for his wife, placing her needs above his own. In the Christian tradition, the husband was to love his wife as Christ loved the church and gave himself up for her. The wife fulfilled a life-giving, nurturing, and homemaking role. In coming together in matrimony, the two not only were able to meet each other's needs, but they also created an essence—a reality greater than the sum of its parts—enabling the couple to serve a higher purpose that transcended their own parochial interests.

Most feminists in the nineteenth century did not seek to overturn this understanding of family order; they merely sought to win recognition within the legal sphere for the intrinsic equality of women and men. Some feminists, however, objected to the traditional understanding of the marriage relationship, maintaining that it was by nature oppressive.

A Selective Reading of Scripture

Elizabeth Cady Stanton and others, for example, wrote *The Woman's Bible*, a series of commentaries that sharply criticized what she considered the position of women in sacred Scripture, in 1895. Blaming the Holy Bible for the lowly status of women, Mrs. Stanton concluded of a woman's lot:

> Marriage for her was to be a condition of bondage, maternity a period of suffering and anguish, and in silence and subjection, she was to play the role of a dependent on man's bounty for all her material wants, and for all the information she might desire on the vital questions of the hour, she was commanded to ask her husband at home.

Mrs. Stanton's reading of Scripture was selective at best, avoiding discussion of texts that would support women's rights and concerns. She could have easily appealed to Proverbs 31, a text that extols the hard-working, intelligent wife engaged in economic activity and praised by husband and children—hardly the sentimental, passive woman of the Victorian era—to support the goals of married women's property acts being passed in many states.

While the National American Women Suffrage Association censured Mrs. Stanton for fear that her best-selling, vitriolic attack on the Bible would jeopardize national suffrage, the women's movement would eventually adopt her hostile stance to traditional religious teaching. Consequently, the feminist movement has brought confusion to many a husband and wife trying to make their marriages work. Told that the complementary roles they formerly exercised are outdated, husbands and wives are encouraged to share their respective responsibilities in the name of equality. Consequently, two people do two jobs halfway, neither meeting the other's needs, while no one is held accountable for a specific set of responsibilities. Further, the perception of interchangeability between man and woman has led to a number of socially destructive conclusions. If men and women are not really any different, then maybe only one parent is necessary or maybe two parents of the same sex might offer an acceptable arrangement. If one parent can do the job, a father may feel no remorse if he abandons his family when the going gets tough, since he offers no unique role in the household anyway. In these subtle ways, the downplaying of the unique roles of men and women contributes to greater public acceptance of divorce and single parenthood while lending credence to the notion of homosexual "unions."

Challenging the Permanence of Marriage

The feminist assault on marriage goes much deeper than simply the blurring of roles. Feminists have also challenged the permanence of marriage through no-fault divorce, which has eroded the nature of marriage by reducing it to an unenforceable contract terminable by either party at will. Supported by feminists ostensibly to protect women by making it easier to leave abusive husbands, no-fault divorce has simply empowered men to abandon their wives and children, increasing the divorce rate and the number of children who suffer growing up in broken homes. The consequences are severe: children of divorce face greater risk of being physically abused and are much more likely than children in intact families to fall into a wide range of deviant behaviors; fatherless children are twice as likely to drop out of school; young children in broken homes are almost five times as likely to live in poverty; and three out of four teenage suicides occur in single-parent households. The likelihood that a young male will engage in criminal activity doubles if he is raised without a father and triples if he lives in a neighborhood with a high concentration of single-parent families.

Feminists and Marriage

• Marriage has long figured as a target of feminist reformers.

• Since the early 1960s, second-wave feminists have campaigned to secure women's complete freedom from marriage.

• The feminist campaigns gave the clear impression that the liberation of women required their liberation from children.

• Marriages must be grounded in the subordination of husband and wife to one another, and of both to the nonnegotiable needs of children.

• In attacking marriage and the family as the wellsprings of civil and political order, feminists are attacking the health of society as a whole.

World & I, November 1997.

Finally, by encouraging mothers to work outside the home, feminism has reaped the tragedy of institutional daycare, diminishing family esteem by advancing the notion that a paid attendant can replicate maternal love and nurture. Institutional day-care is a far greater tragedy than most Americans realize; an on-site visit to a center will confirm to many that there is no place like home. Children are crammed into day-care centers, sometimes with staff-to-child ratios twice as high as those recommended by the National Association for the Education of Young Children, which are one-to-four for babies and one-to-seven for three-year-olds. Because staff turnover is high, children do not develop long-term relationships with the adults responsible for their daily needs. This diminishes not only a child's security but also the ability of adults around him to respond in uniquely appropriate ways to the development of his needs, interests, and personality. With so few caregivers serving so many children, providing children the same amount of time and attention as a one-on-one relationship with a mother at home is impossible.

Increasing the Size and Scope of Government

By weakening the family unit, feminism has directly contributed to [an] increase of social problems . . . ; at the same time, it has diminished the family and society's ability to cope with those problems. Exacerbated by feminism's success at persuading the public that "the personal is political" and thus government is the answer to every problem, the feminist legacy has precipitated an enormous increase in the size and scope of the state. Increased crime rates demand government attention; poverty, poor schooling, and illegitimacy create dependency on the welfare state.

Even intact families have become increasingly dependent on government. Dual-income families press for federal child-care subsidies and even expect schools to provide breakfast as well as lunch. President Clinton called for classifying parents as a protected class in employment discrimination matters in order to help people balance work and family. As mothers neglect their responsibilities in the home, government is more than ready to intervene to fill the void, making sure that business pays the price of their ambitions. Furthermore, without proper examples or role models in the home, children do not grow into adulthood with an understanding of the meaning of order and authority nor do they understand its proper limits. Lacking confidence in the ability of family to meet its members' needs, the public becomes susceptible to demagoguery and an intrusive, paternalistic state that presumes to be better able to provide care.

"Feminists envision a variety of ideal families, not just one."

Feminism Supports the Family

Phyllis Chesler

Widespread charges that feminists are "anti-family" are simply false, argues Phyllis Chesler in the following viewpoint. Feminists clearly support families, Chesler maintains, but have a nontraditional vision of what an ideal family entails. In the view of feminists, states Chesler, families can be made up of friends, same-sex partners, or men and women; however, feminist families differ from the traditional patriarchal family in that they have less sex-role stereotyping, less authoritarianism, and more sharing of both household and economic tasks. In addition, Chesler warns that the institution of marriage can actually hinder people from finding love, respect, and security, and is often dangerous for women and their children. Chesler is the author of *Letters to a Young Feminist*, from which the following viewpoint is excerpted.

As you read, consider the following questions:

1. According to Chesler, what type of families are feminists interested in creating?
2. What is the societal message about marriage, as explained by the author?
3. What evidence does Chesler provide to support her view that throughout history marriage has been "a forced, economic arrangement"?

Feminists have repeatedly been denounced as being anti-family. This is not true. Feminists oppose the patriarchal family that is male-dominated, father-absent, and mother-blaming. There are some good patriarchal families: you're lucky if you come from one. Unfortunately, there are as many families in which children are physically and psychologically disfigured in such a way that they are likely to re-visit such abuse on their own children. Mothers and fathers have, traditionally, enforced gender stereotyping and gender apartheid.

The Feminist Ideal

The feminist ideal—and it is just that, an ideal—is a more egalitarian one. Feminists envision a variety of ideal families, not just one. People sometimes create families with friends; such families are usually not legally recognized, although they may be legally penalized. A family with children may consist of a man and a woman, both, one, or none of whom may be biologically related to the children. A family with children may also consist of same-sex adult pairs, men and women, both, one, or none of whom may be the stay-at-home primary caregiver.

I know two adult lesbians who have chosen to be surrogate grandmothers to the son and daughter of a lesbian couple. They take their responsibilities seriously, baby-sit regularly, celebrate holidays together. As far as I know, there are no screaming scenes, no drunkenness, no sudden unilateral withdrawals.

The way the experience of "family" ought to be, but often isn't.

I know some grandparents who function as their grandchildren's parents—but who are also the elders of an extended family consisting of adoptive, foster, and biological children.

I know a heterosexual woman who, for years, has cultivated the children of her friends. She is blessed with many children.

What Feminist Families Have in Common

What such families often have in common is less sex-role stereotyping, less authoritarianism, and more sharing of both household and economic tasks.

I believe that every citizen—no, every human being—

should be entitled to health and pension coverage whether they are legally married or parents or not. We should not have to "pair up" with one other person to be entitled to certain benefits.

Despite the way feminists have been portrayed in the media, feminists understand that women, like men, long for human connectedness and stability—but rarely have it. Traditional men rarely undertake the work of making relationships or family work. Housekeeping, child care, holiday making, and keeping in touch are what women do for others, not what others in the family do for women—not even for those women who also earn outside money.

Feminists are interested in creating families that do not overburden any one member, economically or domestically. While one's ability to sacrifice certain things for the sake of others is what civilization should be about, a feminist family model is not one based upon the unilateral sacrifice of women only.

The Loneliness of Marriage

The feminists of my generation were the ones who discovered how lonely and isolated many married mothers of young children—and grown children—really were. We discovered that wives (husbands too) are often both sexually and emotionally deprived within marriage—especially when they have young children. Fathers usually had an easier time of getting their egos and sexual needs met elsewhere. Mothers—rarely.

In my view, children need more than one or two parents; adults need more than a mate, however wonderful that mate may be. We all need an extended family—a network of people who will extend themselves to each other. Often, and for a variety of reasons, extended family no longer works in its biological form, i.e., aunts, uncles, grandparents. If we want one—we must often create it for ourselves. . . .

Marriage: A Not-So-Sacred Institution

Marriage as we know it is not likely to disappear anytime soon. But it is certainly not a feminist institution. I do not oppose your right to choose to marry. I do oppose your going into it blindly.

By now, you've no doubt gotten the societal message: If you don't marry, you'll be doomed to a life of loneliness. No one will love you. People will think you're unnatural; selfish too. You will deny your parents and your tribe their earned, genetic immortality, and yourself the joys of children. You will have no one to grow old with, no one who'll remember you when you were young. *God* wants you to marry. Oh, and try to marry a rich man or woman, you can learn to love them just as well.

The Reality of Traditional Families

Admirers of . . . 1950s family forms and values point out that household arrangements and gender roles were less diverse in the 1950s than today, and marriages more stable. But this was partly because diversity was ruthlessly suppressed and partly because economic and political support systems for socially-sanctioned families were far more generous than they are today. Real wages rose more in any single year of the 1950s than they did in the entire decade of the 1980s; the average thirty-year-old man could buy a median-priced home on 15 to 18 percent of his income. The government funded public investment, home ownership, and job creation at a rate more than triple that of the past two decades, while 40 percent of young men were eligible for veteran's benefits. Forming and maintaining families was far easier than it is today.

Yet the stability of these 1950s families did not guarantee good outcomes for their members. Even though most births occurred within wedlock, almost a third of American children lived in poverty during the 1950s, a higher figure than today. More than 50 percent of black married-couple families were poor. Women were often refused the right to serve on juries, sign contracts, take out credit cards in their own names, or establish legal residence. Wife-battering rates were low, but that was because wife-beating was seldom counted as a crime. Most victims of incest, such as Miss America of 1958, kept the secret of their fathers' abuse until the 1970s or 1980s, when the women's movement became powerful enough to offer them the support denied them in the 1950s.

Stephanie Coontz, *National Forum*, September 1, 1996.

Let my voice be heard above this barrage of propaganda. At the very least, I would like you to think about marriage before you enter into it. I never did.

No one tells you that marriage *as we know it* may actually stand in the way of what we most want from it: love, passion, respect, security, stability, continuity, growth. No one ever told me that, far from being the solution, patriarchal marriage is exceptionally dangerous for women and their children. Sometimes, a private home is the most dangerous place for a woman to be.

If, as feminist women and men, you want to create unions that are stable, felicitous, and egalitarian, you may have to forget nearly everything that you've been so carefully taught. You literally can't afford to marry or have marriage-like relationships with anyone. I am not saying you cannot love or live with each other; I am saying that you must do so for different reasons and on different terms than anything you've imagined.

Women, especially, can't afford to look for a protector or father-figure: it will do you in. We are all interdependent, but you should only make alliances with peers, not with those who are more powerful than you.

Emma Goldman said she was against marriage too—if for no other reason than it placed crowns of thorns upon the heads of innocent babes and called them bastards if their mothers weren't married.

The Price of Marriage

Also, for every marriage that is made in Heaven, there is a marriage made in Hell. As you know, many marriages do not last, and many that do exact too great a price in exchange. From both men and women. However, divorce is not the solution either. A divorce does not solve our economic problems, or our need for a family and community.

I am not saying that heterosexual men and women can't or shouldn't love each other or live together or create families. Some married folk say they are very happy or happy enough with what they've got, and I have no reason to disbelieve them; some single folks say the same thing. Hear Ye: I am not saying that unmarried people are happier than married people or that impoverished single mothers are better off than a wealthy, two-parent family.

I am saying that, historically, from a feminist point of view, for thousands of years, marriage, as we know it, has been a forced, economic arrangement. On both sides. Legal marriage has often (but not always) isolated women from their families of origin and from bonding with other women, exploited women as indentured (unsalaried) live-in domestic and reproductive servants, and formerly entitled a husband to his wife's wages when she worked outside the home—and to her inheritance too.

Marriage also oppressed women sexually: until recently, a wife could not charge her husband with rape. By definition, she was his sexual and reproductive property. (If a wife alleges marital rape, she must still convince a judge and jury—no easy task.) Marriage also endangered women physically: until very recently, women couldn't allege marital battery. Women are still a long way from ending marital abuse and from winning the right to defend themselves. A traditional wife was not entitled to time off, or to lovers of her own—although she was expected to forgive her husband for straying.

Not a pretty picture.

If we only have "bad" alternatives, choosing the lesser of two evils may be the best you can do. This does not mean it is a feminist solution. A feminist solution would require finding others who are in your situation, who see things as you do, and who also want to create a feminist marriage or community.

Visible, mainstream, feminist alternatives have yet to be created.

My parents married for life. They did not expect to be happy. Their expectations were fully met. They expected to survive, economically, and to raise children. In this, they were entirely successful.

I never wanted a marriage like that, and I've never had one.

I did, however, marry: not once, but twice. The passion did not last, promises were not kept, my life was endangered. Although no harm was intended, harm was done—on both sides.

I deeply regret this.

Periodical Bibliography

The following articles have been selected to supplement the diverse views presented in this chapter. Addresses are provided for periodicals not indexed in the *Readers' Guide to Periodical Literature*, the *Alternative Press Index*, the *Social Sciences Index*, or the *Index to Legal Periodicals and Books*.

Jay Ambrose	"Casualties at the Feminist Frontier," *Washington Times*, July 6, 1996.
David Brooks	"Our Bodies, Our Surgeons: Feminism in the Age of Body Worship," *Weekly Standard*, February 7, 2000. Available from 1211 Avenue of the Americas, New York, NY 10036.
Midge Decter	"Wedding Bell Blues," *American Outlook*, Spring 1999.
F. Carolyn Graglia	"Feminism Isn't Antisex. It's Only Antifamily," *Wall Street Journal*, August 6, 1998.
Joseph Perkins	"Revamped Rules of Romance," *Washington Times*, June 10, 1997.
Paul Craig Roberts	"Casualties of the Sexual Revolution," *Conservative Chronicle*, August 11, 1999. Available from 9 Second St. NW, Hampton, IA 50441.
Cathy Young	"Conservative Confusion on Feminism," *New Republic*, April 12, 1999.

Is Feminism Obsolete?

Chapter Preface

In March 1999, *USA Today* reported that, according to a recent Gallup poll, only 26 percent of American women over the age of eighteen consider themselves feminists. Feminist scholars and media commentators have offered a variety of perspectives on why women's support for feminism appears to be dwindling. One argument is that radical feminist tenets—especially the belief that women are victimized by men—have alienated some women. Elinor Burkett, author of *The Right Women: A Journey Through the Heart of Conservative America*, writes,

> Ultimately, American women have rejected the feminist movement . . . because they sense that the movement doesn't really like or respect women. . . . The [feminist] movement holds women to impossibly high, and absurdly narrow, standards and gives them no credit for being able to forge their separate peace, treating them precisely as disapproving men have been wont to do. It . . . demeans their intelligence by bemoaning most of their decisions as still further evidence that they are victims.

Others maintain that women's reluctance to call themselves feminists is the result of conservatives' portrayals of feminists as strident, man-hating "femi-nazis." Common caricatures of feminists are so derogatory, some argue, that women feel compelled to disassociate themselves from the labels "feminist" or "feminism." As writer Garry Wills points out, many women who claim they are not feminists state that they support the women's movement. In the same Gallup poll reported by *USA Today*, 87 percent of the respondents agreed that the women's movement will be important in the twenty-first century. In a recent Harris poll, although only half of the women polled identified themselves as feminists, 71 percent said that they advocated "political, economic, and social equality for women."

Although women may support the ideals of feminism, the question of whether feminism continues to be a viable political and social force remains unanswered. In the chapter that follows, authors offer contrasting opinions on whether the feminist movement has become obsolete.

"Feminism today is wed to the culture of celebrity and self-obsession."

The Feminist Movement Is Dead

Ginia Bellafante

Ginia Bellafante, a writer for *Time* magazine, maintains in the following viewpoint that the feminist movement, once a political and social movement that sought equal rights and opportunities for women, has devolved into an elite culture of women who are interested in little else than celebrity, sex, and themselves. Furthermore, Bellafante argues, issues of true importance to American women, such as day care, are virtually ignored by feminist icons and organizations. Feminism as a political force is dead, she concludes.

As you read, consider the following questions:
1. In Bellafante's opinion, how is the feminism of today different from that of the '60s and '70s?
2. Why is "the flightiness of contemporary feminism" a problem, according to Bellafante?
3. What is the "Camille Paglia syndrome," in the words of the author?

Growing up in Washington state during the '70s, Courtney Love didn't care much for the women's-movement rallies her mother attended. "I'd wonder why nobody on these marches was wearing heels," she has said. But with its days of flat shoes and fiery protest behind it, feminism is clearly more attractive to Love now. Earlier this year, the angry rocker turned Versace model and movie star showed up at the *Ms.* Foundation's 25th-anniversary bash at Caroline's Comedy Club in New York City. A busy celebrity, she couldn't stay long. Springing up to leave midway through the event, she announced, "Can you believe it? Here I am with Gloria Steinem, and now I'm off to dinner with Milos Forman!"

The *Ms.* party was one of many in a hectic season of feminist nightlife in Manhattan. In April 1998 came Show, a living work of art by Vanessa Beecroft designed to humanize media images of female beauty and thus somehow invest women with power. The invitees gathered in the rotunda of the Guggenheim Museum in Manhattan to view 15 bikini-clad models staring into space atop their high heels. But the glitziest affair . . . was a reading of *The Vagina Monologues,* a performance piece about female private parts by Eve Ensler that attracted Uma Thurman, Winona Ryder and Calista Flockhart, among others. The actresses had come to raise money to fight domestic violence, but the cause seemed lost amid the event's giddy theatrics. Featured were Marisa Tomei on the subject of pubic hair (sample line: "You cannot love a vagina unless you love hair"); Glenn Close offering an homage to an obscene word for female genitalia; and, finally, the playwright delivering three solid minutes of orgasmic moaning. The *Village Voice* called it "the most important and outrageous feminist event" of the past 30 years.

Fashion spectacle, paparazzi-jammed galas, mindless sex talk—is this what the road map to greater female empowerment has become? If feminism is, as Gloria Steinem has said for decades, "a revolution and not a public relations movement," why has it come to feel so much like spin?

Steinem isn't the person to answer that question. The doyen of second-wave feminism startled many in March 1998 when she penned an op-ed piece for the *New York Times* arguing that the allegations of a sexual dalliance between the President and a 21-year-old intern were nothing to get worked up about. If the stories were true (and she believed they were), then Clinton was guilty of nothing more than frat boyishness, Steinem wrote. *Backlash* author Susan Faludi also made excuses for the President, writing in the *Nation* that along with other powers, women have gained "the power to forgive men." And in the places where you would expect feminist indignation to be thriving—the elite liberal colleges of the Northeast—*Time* found in numerous interviews that it isn't. On the Clinton sex scandal, Barnard College senior Rebecca Spence says, "As a self-defined feminist, I should be outraged, but I'm not."

Conservatives have an easy explanation for these forgiving attitudes toward the President's private treatment of women. They say Clinton-loving feminists, as if following the how-to-catch-a-man *Rules* manual, have chosen to overlook the faults of a man who has been their best provider. Ideals be damned for the President who vetoed the ban on partial-birth abortions.

But political allegiance is only part of the story. If women's leaders seemed to ignore some of the murkier questions raised by the Clinton scandal—for example, what does consensual sex mean between two people so unequal in power?—it is in part because feminism at the very end of the century seems to be an intellectual undertaking in which the complicated, often mundane issues of modern life get little attention and the narcissistic ramblings of a few new media-anointed spokeswomen get far too much. You'll have better luck becoming a darling of feminist circles if you chronicle your adventures in cybersex than if you churn out a tome on the glass ceiling.

What a comedown for the movement. If women were able to make their case in the '60s and '70s, it was largely because, as the slogan went, they turned the personal into the political. They used their daily experience as the basis for a critique, often a scholarly one, of larger institutions and social arrangements. From Simone de Beauvoir's *Second Sex* to Betty Friedan's *Feminine Mystique* to Kate Millett's *Sexual Politics*—a doctoral dissertation that became a national best seller—feminists made big, unambiguous demands of the world. They sought absolute equal rights and opportunities for women, a constitutional amendment to make it so, a chance to be compensated equally and to share the task of raising a family. But if feminism of the '60s and '70s was steeped in research and obsessed with social change, feminism today is wed to the culture of celebrity and self-obsession.

It is fair to ask why anyone should be worried about this outcome. Who cares about the trivial literary and artistic pursuits of a largely Manhattan-based group of self-appointed feminists? They're talking only to one another, after all. But the women's movement, like many upheavals before it, from the French Revolution in 1789 to the civil rights movement in the U.S. and even the uprising in Tiananmen Square, would be nowhere without the upper-middle-class intellectual elite. Feminism didn't start in the factory. It started in wood-paneled salons, spread to suburban living rooms, with their consciousness-raising sessions, and eventually ended up with Norma Rae. In fact, that trajectory is its biggest problem today—it remains suspect to those who have never ventured onto a college campus. A *Time/CNN* poll shows what most people already suspect—that education more than anything else determines whether a woman defines herself as a feminist. Fifty-three percent of white, college-educated women living in cities embrace the label. Fifty percent of white women with postgraduate training and no children do the same. But feminism shouldn't be punished for its pedigree. We would never have had Ginger Spice if we hadn't had Germaine Greer.

And that brings up another reason why the flightiness of contemporary feminism is a problem. Some would argue that if the women's movement were still useful, it would have something to say; it's dead because it has won. Some wags have coined a phrase for this: Duh Feminism. But there's nothing obvious about the movement's achievements. It's true that we now have a woman crafting America's foreign policy (Madeleine Albright), that a woman is deciding which Barbie dolls to produce (Jill Barad, CEO of Mattel) and that a woman (Catharine MacKinnon) pioneered the field of sexual-harassment law (which is turning into real dollars for real women, as Mitsubishi Motors evidenced . . . with its record $34 million payment to women on the assembly line). It's also true that women are joining together for their own, big-draw rock tours and that we now have "girl power," that sassy, don't-mess-with-me adolescent spirit that Madison Avenue carefully caters to. So yes, the women's movement changed our individual lives and expectations, and young women today acknowledge this. A hefty 50% of those from ages 18 to 34 told the pollsters in the *Time/CNN* survey that they share "feminist" values, by which they generally mean they want a world in which they can choose to be any-thing—the President or a mother, or both.

But that doesn't mean that American society is supporting them much in their choices, and this is where the pseudo-feminists of today could be of help. The average female worker in America still earns just 76 cents for every dollar a man earns, up 17 cents from the '70s but still no cause for re-joicing. And for most women, the glass ceiling is as impene-trable as ever. There are only two female CEOs at Fortune 500 companies, and just 10% of corporate officers are women. Day care, a top priority for both middle-class women and less fortunate mothers maneuvering through welfare reform, still seems a marginal issue to feminist leaders. Under the heading Key Issues on the website of the National Organization for Women, day care isn't even mentioned.

Instead, much of feminism has devolved into the silly. And it has powerful support for this: a popular culture insistent on offering images of grown single women as frazzled, self-absorbed girls. Ally McBeal is the most popular female char-acter on television. The show, for the few who may have missed it, focuses on a ditsy 28-year-old Ivy League Boston litigator who never seems in need of the body-concealing clothing that Northeastern weather often requires. Ally spends much of her time fantasizing about her ex-boyfriend, who is married and in the next office, and manages to work references to her mangled love life into nearly every sum-mation she delivers. She has fits in supermarkets because there are too few cans of Pringles. She answers the question "Why are your problems so much bigger than everyone else's?" with the earnest response "Because they're mine." When Ally gets any work done, how she keeps her job, why she thinks it's O.K. to ask her secretary why she didn't give her a birthday present—these are all mysteries. Ally probably wouldn't seem so offensive as an addition to the cast of Seinfeld, but because this is a one-hour drama filled with pseudo–Melissa Etheridge music and emotional pretense, we are meant to take her problems more seriously than George Costanza's. "Ally McBeal is a mess. She's like a little animal," notes Nancy Friday, a sex-positive feminist if ever there was one. "You want to put her on a leash." And what does Ally's creator David Kelley have to say about Ally as a feminist? "She's not a hard, strident feminist out of the '60s and '70s. She's all for women's rights, but she doesn't want to lead the charge at her own emotional expense." Ally, though, is in charge of nothing, least of all her emotional life. . . .

Ally McBeal . . . [is] the product of what could be called the Camille Paglia syndrome. In her landmark 1990 book, *Sexual Personae*, author Paglia used intellect to analyze art, history and literature from classical times to the 19th century and argue that it is men who are the weaker sex because they have remained eternally powerless over their desire for the female body. It is female sexuality, she said, that is humanity's greatest force. Her tome helped catapult feminism beyond an ideology of victimhood.

In the heated atmosphere of early-'90s gender politics, in which Anita Hill accused Clarence Thomas of sexual harassment before an audience of millions, Paglia quickly began turning up all over the media voicing her controversial opinions on the sex wars. Feminism wasted time trying to persuade us that men are tameable, she proclaimed. Relish sexual power, she told women, but don't go to frat parties expecting men to be saints. The argument was powerful and full of merit, but deployed by lesser minds it quickly devolved into an excuse for media-hungry would-be feminists to share their adventures in the mall or in bed. So let us survey the full post-Paglia landscape.

Out [in] spring 1998 was Lisa Palac's *The Edge of the Bed*, in which the author suggests that pornography can be liberating because X-rated movies were sexually freeing for her. "Once I figured out how to look at an erotic image and use my sexual imagination to turn desire into a self-generated orgasm, my life was irrevocably and positively changed," writes Palac. The subtext of her book is that sexual self-revelation is groundbreaking in itself. But of course it isn't. It's at least as old as the '70s. That decade gave us, among other things, the erotic art of feminist group-sex advocate Betty Dodson and a NOW-sponsored sexuality conference that covered the subject of sadomasochism. And it gave us Erica Jong's titillating *Fear of Flying*, as well as Nancy Friday's 1973 best seller, *My Secret Garden*, which celebrated female sexual fantasies.

A *Time/CNN* Poll on Feminism

Is feminism today relevant to most women?

Women who answered yes	48%
Feminists who answered yes	64%
Nonfeminists who answered yes	42%

Is feminism relevant to you personally?

Women who answered yes	28%
Feminists who answered yes	58%
Nonfeminists who answered yes	16%

Do feminists share your values?

Women	Yes	No
18–34	50%	39%
35–49	41%	44%
50–64	42%	45%
65+	27%	49%

What is your impression of feminists?

	1989	1998
Favorable	44%	32%
Unfavorable	29%	43%

Beyond Palac, there are other young postfeminists who have launched careers by merely plucking from and personalizing Paglia's headline-making ideas. The latest addition to the women's-studies sections of bookstores, *Bitch: In Praise of Difficult Women*, features on its cover a topless picture of author Elizabeth Wurtzel. Beyond it lies a seemingly unedited rant in which Wurtzel, billed on her book jacket as a Pagliaite, demands for herself and womankind the right to be rapacious, have fits and own more than one Gucci bag. "I intend to scream, shout, throw tantrums in Bloomingdale's if I feel like it and confess intimate details of my life to complete strangers," she writes. "I intend to answer only to myself."

Then there is 29-year-old Katie Roiphe, who appeared on the scene with her 1993 book, *The Morning After*, arguing that heightened date-rape awareness on college campuses was creating a culture of sexual fear and hysteria. She has gone on to write articles that excuse bad male behavior and tout her own desirability. In a piece that appeared in the January 1998 issue of *Vogue*, she told the story of an affair she had had with a teacher when she was 16. "In that first moment of thinking, maybe he likes me, there is a blossoming of feminine power," she wrote. "I remember first learning from my 36-year-old teacher that I had the ability to attract a man." The implication is that such relationships empower young girls because this one, she feels, was good for her. (Roiphe is currently expressing her feminine power as a model for Coach leather goods.)

The most fussed-about young poet of the moment is Deborah Garrison, whose new collection, *A Working Girl Can't Win*, revolves around a quintessentially self-absorbed postfeminist. Again we get a picture of a career woman in her 20s who doesn't feel pretty enough and who fantasizes about life as a sexpot. "I'm never going to sleep/ with Martin Amis/ or anyone famous./ At twenty-one I scotched/my chance to be/one of the seductresses/of the century,/ a vamp on the rise through the ranks/ of literary Gods and military men,/ who wouldn't stop at the President:/ she'd take the Pentagon by storm/ in halter dress and rhinestone extras," Garrison writes in "An Idle Thought." (It could be retitled "Oh, How I Would Have Put You to Shame, Monica Lewinsky.") Garrison's efforts won her a book blurb from feminist columnist Katha Pollitt, who described the poems as "brave, elegant, edgy."

Even those feminists who don't necessarily embrace Paglia's world view seem to have inherited the postfeminist tic of offering up autobiography as theory. A 1995 anthology of young feminist thought, *To Be Real*, compiled by Rebecca Walker, is a collection of airy—sometimes even ludicrous—mini-memoirs meant to expand our understanding of female experience. She introduces the material by explaining that she first felt guilty about putting together such an introspective, apolitical book. But, Walker says, she resisted the pressure "to make a book I really wasn't all that desperate to read." An essay by Veena Cabreros-Sud tells us how empowering it can be to have random fistfights with strangers. And there's the interview with model Veronica Webb titled "How Does a Supermodel Do Feminism?", in which she explains that while the fashion industry may make women feel inadequate, there is a physically deformed little girl she knows "who actually has more self-confidence than I do."

Feminist author Naomi Wolf's most recent book, 1997's *Promiscuities*, draws on what she and her friends experienced growing up to make the point that female longing is dangerously suppressed in our culture. She argues that the world would be a better place if we celebrated women's sexuality the way so many ancient peoples did. "Confucius, in his Book of Rites," she writes, "held that it was a husband's duty to take care of his wife or concubine sexually as well as financially and emotionally." It seems to have eluded Wolf that ancient Chinese women might have aspired to something better than life as a concubine.

Then there is the matter of *Bust*, the hip magazine of the moment. Created by Debbie Stoller, a 35-year-old who holds a doctorate in women's studies from Yale, and Marcelle Karp, a 34-year-old TV producer, *Bust* is a magazine intentionally written in teenspeak but meant for female readers in their late 20s and early 30s. It was developed as an antidote to magazines like *Cosmopolitan*, which present female sexuality so cartoonishly. However noble the intent, the message is often lost in the magazine's adolescent tone: read about an adult woman's first-time vibrator discoveries or a scintillating account of lust for delivery men in an article titled "Sex with the UPS Guy." Of the magazine's purposely immature tone, Stoller says, "Women have been forced into roles as women and now they're rebelling." But in the end, *Bust* offers a peekaboo view of the world of sex that leaves one feeling not like an empowered adult but more like a 12-year-old sneaking in some sexy reading behind her parents' back.

Bust, which began as a photocopied 'zine, is essentially a product of alternative culture's Riot Grrrl movement, an effort by new female bands in the early '90s to reclaim the brash, bratty sense of self-control that psychologists claim girls lose just before puberty. And in many ways, the movement succeeded, as any fan of Sleater-Kinney and even the Spice Girls will tell you. But even in the world of pop music, with the spirit of girl power behind it, the concept of feminism is often misapplied. Look how the label is tossed about: female singers like Meredith Brooks and Alanis Morissette are installed as icons of woman power (alongside real artist-activists like Tori Amos) simply because they sing about bad moods or boyfriends who have dumped them. In the late '60s, when the label was applied more sparingly, no one thought to call Nancy Sinatra a feminist, and yet if she recorded "These Boots Are Made for Walkin'" in 1998, she'd probably find herself headlining the Lilith Fair.

Part of the reason for Riot Grrrl's impact is that it often focused on the issue of childhood sexual abuse. Not only did the songs relate harrowing personal experiences but the band members started 'zines and websites through which teenagers who had been molested could communicate with one another. Riot Grrrl's concerns paralleled those of feminists in the grownup world who, around the same time, also became preoccupied with sexual abuse and self-help (even Steinem got in on the act with her 1992 book, *Revolution from Within*). But many of those grownups, who called themselves feminist therapists, ended up attaching themselves to the bizarre fringes of the sexual-recovery movement. "Women weren't looking at their lives and saying, 'I'm stressed because I'm getting no help at home,' they were saying, 'I'm stressed out because my family molested me in the crib,'" explains social psychologist Carol Tavris. "The feelings of powerlessness many women continued to have in the early '90s got attached to sex-abuse-survivor syndrome." When Tavris debunked self-help books on incest-survivor syndrome in the *New York Times Book Review* in

117

1993, she received a flood of letters from feminist therapists calling her a betrayer.

If feminism has come to seem divorced from matters of public purpose, it is thanks in part to shifts in the academy. "Women's studies, a big chunk of it at least, has focused increasingly on the symbols of the body and less on social action and social change," explains Leslie Calman, a political-science professor and director of the Center for Research on Women at Barnard College. Moreover, gender studies, the theoretical analysis of how gender identities are constructed, have become increasingly incorporated into women's studies or turned into rival departments of their own. In April 1998, Yale University renamed its Women's Studies Department the Women and Gender Studies Department.

It's not surprising that Old Guard feminists, surveying their legacy, are dismayed by what they see. "All the sex stuff is stupid," said Betty Friedan. "The real problems have to do with women's lives and how you put together work and family." Says Susan Brownmiller, author of *Against Our Will*, which pioneered the idea that rape is a crime of power: "These are not movement people. I don't know whom they're speaking for. They seem to be making individual bids for stardom." It's easy to dismiss the voices of Old Guard feminists as the typical complaints of leaders nostalgic for their days at center stage. But is Ally McBeal really progress? Maybe if she lost her job and wound up a single mom, we could begin a movement again.

"Feminism in its many forms is continually transforming our lives."

The Feminist Movement Is Not Dead

Part I: Marcia Ann Gillespie; Part II: Carolyn Waldron

In Part I of the following two-part viewpoint, *Ms.* magazine editor Marcia Ann Gillespie counters claims that feminism is "dead" and that contemporary feminists are self-involved. Such claims, she asserts, unfairly portray feminism as a monolithic entity and disregard the ongoing work of disparate groups of feminist activists. In Part II, Carolyn Waldron, a writer for *FAIR* (Fairness and Accuracy in Reporting), argues that media articles heralding the "death of feminism" misrepresent feminism by depicting it in simplistic, stereotypic terms. Instead of constructing caricatures about feminism, Waldron states, the media should work to provide more complete and accurate coverage of the feminist movement.

As you read, consider the following questions:
1. According to Gillespie, what is one important reason why the feminist movement thrives?
2. In Waldron's view, what is the method by which media articles attempt to discredit the feminist movement?

I

S ince feminism's second wave caught hold some three decades ago, every few years a major feature article on the state of the movement is published and heralded as a benchmark piece for the public to debate. Such articles would provide a valuable jumping-off place for public discussion concerning feminism's contributions to society if they provided a genuine characterization. Invariably, however, these articles do more to obfuscate and stall debate—even to move it backwards—than to enlighten. The most recent example is *Time's* 6/29/98 cover story, "Is Feminism Dead?"

Creating a "Straw Woman" of Feminism

These articles follow a similar pattern: First, they construct an arbitrary, stereotypic definition of feminism. Then, the articles ask whether or not this "feminism" is dead. This frame leaves feminist advocates stuck in neutral with no way to move forward; the best we can do is to repeatedly prove the stereotype is false and that the movement is alive. And for antifeminists, each new feature article provides a "straw woman," the newest caricature of feminism to attack, and an ostensibly authoritative new source to quote on the death of feminism.

The stereotypes of feminism presented in these articles have changed over the years, but the means of creating each straw woman remain constant. The predictable formula is to include only the people, events, issues and characterizations that create a simple stereotype of the movement at a given time. For example, *Time* magazine's 1989 cover story "Women Face the Nineties" (12/4/89) conjured up that old familiar masculine stereotype of feminists with the line, "hairy legs haunt the feminist movement, as do images of being strident and lesbian." The piece went on to claim the movement had emphasized the ERA [Equal Rights Amendment] and lesbian rights over "the pressing need for child care."

Typically, a few unrepresentative but famous people are given as examples of feminist leaders, leaving many average and representative activists totally out of the picture. Sally Quinn's representation of Barbara Streisand and Jane Fonda as "hypocritical feminist leaders" in her 1992 *Washington Post* piece "Who Killed Feminism?" (1/19/92), is a case in point.

The new stereotype of feminism appearing in *Time*'s "Is Feminism Dead?" is glamorous, glitzy and sex-crazed. Presented as evidence is the work of authors such as Camille Paglia ("Relish sexual power . . . but don't go to frat parties expecting men to be saints," is *Time*'s paraphrase) and events such as *The Vagina Monologues*, performed by actors Glenn Close and Whoopi Goldberg. Not all of *Time*'s examples even represent feminism; those that do fail to present a complete picture. Just as with the masculine stereotype of feminism, the point is to construct a straw woman who is out of touch with today's real woman.

Beyond Survival

The repeated framing of feminism as a single, narrow entity that is perpetually on its deathbed has severely limited discussion in the mainstream press, and, thus, the information that average citizens have for exploring the subject. A Nexis search reveals hundreds of columns and letters to the editor in daily newspapers and magazines on the subject of whether or not feminism is dead. Most of these pieces explicitly say they are responding to one of the "Is Feminism Dead?" feature articles mentioned above. Those that don't respond directly to one of the major articles still seem compelled to debate the death of feminism, as if viability had to be proven before any other issue could be addressed.

It is long past time to move media coverage and public discussion of feminism beyond the question of movement survival. Feminism in its many forms is continually transforming our lives; it includes many different human faces around the globe, and the public deserves a much fuller account. Media activists can help transform the public debate by aggressively prodding news outlets to provide more complete coverage. Let the next benchmark article on feminism ask, "What are today's diverse strains of feminist thought and political and social action, and how might they be affecting society?"

II

You'd think that the 150th anniversary of the birth of the American women's movement would merit mainstream media attention, considering how far we've come and how much this revolution has transformed society. I hoped that maybe, just maybe, instead of more of the usual antifeminist crap, they'd give credit where credit has been long overdue. What was I thinking?

Instead, up popped *Time* magazine with a cover story asking "Is Feminism Dead?" A question this "news" magazine basically answered right on the cover with purposely drab black and white images of three real women leaders of this movement—Susan B. Anthony, Betty Friedan, and Gloria Steinem—alongside a full-color photo of Calista Flockhart as Ally McBeal, the character she plays on television.

This Modern World by Tom Tomorrow. Used with permission.

In case you didn't get where they were going, the main article—one woman's opinion barely dressed up as news reportage—which never so much as mentioned this historic anniversary, informed readers that feminism was being undone by the self-involved trivial pursuits of feminists. The proof? That Courtney Love attended a *Ms.* Foundation for

Women benefit and that there was a star-studded staging of Eve Ensler's *The Vagina Monologues* this winter. And that disciples of Camille Paglia, whom the *Time* writer considers a real trailblazer (huh?), have misinterpreted and trivialized her message about female sexual power. As if *that* were even possible, considering that Paglia's "feminism" has been all about promoting Camille Paglia by bashing feminists.

But I digress. The fact that claiming one's body and consciously choosing the language used to describe it is part of feminism seems to have eluded *Time*. I guess they missed that part. Just like they obscured the fact that the celebrity reading of *The Vagina Monologues,* a work raved about by feminist and nonfeminist critics alike, wasn't an exercise in ego masturbation by the participants but a benefit for those working to end domestic violence—an issue first raised by feminists.

Ignoring Feminist Activism

The more I read, the more I shook my head. Young women's activism was totally ignored, as if the Spice Girls were the epitome of "girl power." No mention of [folk-rock singer] Nomy Lamm, or [musician] Ani DiFranco, organizations like Third Wave, or interviews with any of the many women of that generation who are doing righteous work. Feminists of color didn't even make *Time*'s radar screen—but then we never do. Nor did all the ongoing, change-making work of feminists of all ages, classes, and ethnicities.

For example, according to *Time*, the National Organization for Women's Web site did not include child care in its list of major concerns (NOW denies this), and based on this disputed finding, the writer ignored all the work being done by feminists on this issue and concluded that we just don't care.

Not too long ago, feminism was being castigated for focusing on women's victimization, as if breaking silence about sexual harassment, violence, abuse, and exploitation; challenging centuries of woman-blaming; and demanding justice was nothing more than a pity party. Then . . . we were being chided by many in the media for *not* doing the "victim feminism" thing by failing to rally around Paula Jones and denounce Bill Clinton as a sexual harasser. (As if they ever *really* asked us what we think.) Twenty-five years ago we were supposedly too serious; now the news, according to *Time*, is that "much of feminism has devolved into the silly."

Feminist Supporters Have Kept on Steppin'

Since the first women's rights convention was held in 1848, this movement has been declared dead, dying, or doomed to failure every step along the way. Meanwhile, its supporters have kept on steppin'—some wearing high heels and some clad in combat boots. Challenging the culture and practice of patriarchy happens on many fronts, takes many forms, and encompasses a range of passions. The way one woman expresses her feminism may cause other feminists to applaud, cringe, or rail against her. That was true 150 years ago, and it's true now. One of the many reasons why this movement thrives is because of its ability to allow for difference, to encompass the idiosyncratic and iconoclastic.

"Silly"? Yes, we've been called that many times before; "shocking," "irrelevant," and "elitist," too. There's something comforting about the fact that in 150 years the antifeminist vocabulary hasn't changed much. Especially since, despite the torrent of words churned out to mock, demean, or dismiss our movement, it still comes down to this: feminism has changed women's—and men's—lives for the better. Young women have choices and opportunities that they take for granted, but that would not exist if it weren't for feminism. And most women in this country are grateful that feminists stand up for their rights, even if they themselves can't or won't.

If Ally McBeal is proof that feminism's gone self-centered and silly, then where's the *Time* cover about patriarchy featuring Beavis and Butt-head?

| "The reason the feminist cause is
irretrievably damaged . . . is that its
erstwhile champions have no arguments."

Feminism Has Abandoned Its Original Principles

Charles Krauthammer

In the viewpoint that follows, Charles Krauthammer contends that the refusal of prominent feminists to condemn
Bill Clinton's behavior toward Paula Jones, Monica Lewinsky, and Juanita Broaddrick is hypocritical in light of prior
feminist attacks on Republican leaders accused of far less serious offenses. The feminist reaction to the Clinton scan-
dals, Krauthammer maintains, is clear proof that feminism
has no authentic principles about issues of workplace sex,
sexual harassment, and rape. Krauthammer is a contributing
editor to the *Weekly Standard*, a conservative magazine.

As you read, consider the following questions:

1. According to Krauthammer, what was one of the major
   tenets of feminism prior to the Monica Lewinsky scandal?
2. How did feminists respond to the sexual harassment suit
   put forth by Paula Jones, as explained by the author?
3. As cited by the author, what remarks did the president of
   the National Organization for Women, Patricia Ireland,
   make about Juanita Broaddrick?

Reprinted from "Defining Feminism Down," by Charles Krauthammer, *The
Weekly Standard*, March 15, 1999. Reprinted by permission of the author.

Like the careless Buchanans of *The Great Gatsby*, Bill Clinton is known as the man who leaves friends wounded and bleeding in his wake. But of all the casualties littering his trail—the jailed business partners, the disgraced aides, the character-assassinated former lovers—the most serious by far is feminism: Feminist leaders, feminist groups, feminist ideology, and the Democratic party, once the party of women and women's rights, will never recover.

Consider:

(a) Before Monica Lewinsky, it was a major tenet of feminism and an increasingly accepted workplace ethic that even consensual sex involving a subordinate and the boss was suspect given the unequal power relationship and the potential for exploitation. That was then.

Now, the most powerful man in the world, but fatefully a Democrat, has an affair at work with a 21-year-old intern, an affair exploitative in the extreme. (Remember: The president's *defense*—against charges of perjury—was that in every single encounter he'd merely been serviced without any reciprocation.) And what happens? The man's feminist and Democratic allies attack those looking into the affair for violating the man's privacy.

The New Feminist Principle on Workplace Sex

New feminist principle: Even workplace sex is private. And the inquisitors who violate that privacy are guilty of "sexual McCarthyism."

(b) Before Paula Jones, it was a major tenet of feminism and an increasingly accepted workplace ethic that the degradation and objectification of women—even giving away a nude calendar as a year-end bonus—could contribute to a "hostile work environment" and constitute sexual harassment. That was then.

Well, if cheesecake on the wall can violate women, how about the boss summoning an employee, dropping his pants, and instructing her to kiss it? Pretty serious. Just the kind of behavior women's groups and the Democratic party crusade against.

Why, when Clarence Thomas was accused of nothing much more than some off-color remarks—no exposing, no touching, no groping, no servicing, nothing of the sort—Barbara Boxer led a delegation of House Democratic women who stormed the Senate demanding his head. That was then.

This time around, feminists disdained the woman seeking redress (Paula Jones), and Democrats joined the White House in savaging her. It's just "he said, she said," you see. Who you gonna believe? The Oxford-Yale man or trailer trash?

(c) Before the Jones deposition, it was a major tenet of feminism and an accepted principle of civil procedure, that in a sexual harassment suit the past sexual habits of the accused predator should be open to legal inquiry. That was then.

When it turned out that Bill Clinton lied repeatedly under oath in the Paula Jones suit, the feminists were silent, and the Democratic party waged a vigorous campaign to minimize the offense, arguing—and voting—that lying about sex is not really perjury, that it is only to be expected and, besides, this is an area of privacy that the man should never have been made to testify about in the first place.

A New Stance on Rape

(d) Before Juanita Broaddrick, it was a major tenet of feminism that rape was a serious charge. A plausible charge of rape leveled against a public figure—even a boxer like Mike Tyson—would bring indignant demands for an accounting and for justice. The *Rashomon* dodge—"who can ever really know"—was considered the last refuge of scoundrels. That was then.

Now, Juanita Broaddrick, a woman of maturity and character and with no discernible ulterior motive, says that Bill Clinton raped her in 1978—and all is silence.

National Organization for Women president Patricia Ireland says that, yes, Juanita Broaddrick's story is troubling, but it only highlights how conservatives have been blocking needed changes in legislation on hate crimes and violence against women, and other some such in the Congress. This changing of the subject is hilariously akin to President Clinton responding to charges of massive campaign finance law violations by urging the passage of yet new laws.

The "Let's Move On" Position

But the bankruptcy of the feminist position was best illustrated by Susan Estrich, a leading Democratic figure, stridently defending the "let's move on" position by invoking her authority as herself "a rape victim." She used to invoke that authority to call for moving in on the victimizer. The Democratic party is certainly a gloat-free zone today. You could see not only discomfort but actual shame in the face of Democrats who, having made careers of defending women's rights and protesting their abuse, must now dismiss a rape charge, not with a denial but with shoulder-shrugging agnosticism. Democratic leaders Dick Gephardt and Tom Daschle, evincing not the slightest curiosity as to whether their leader is a rapist, say that it is time for the country to "put this behind us" and "move on" to more important business.

Feminism Is a Political Special Interest Group

What principle could enable the National Organization for Women to continue to support a President who is certainly as much a sexual harasser as [Supreme Court Justice] Clarence Thomas? None. But this President provided NOW with appointments like Norma Cantu in the Department of Education, who places the most expansive interpretation on definitions of discrimination and harassment. These expansive definitions, in turn, create numerous opportunities for feminist attorneys to generate cases and earn legal fees. NOW, in essence, is in the business of supporting feminist ambulance-chasing. Clinton signs legislation that creates jobs in rape crisis centers, battered women's shelters and sensitivity-training centers. In short, he provides pork barrel projects.

Jennifer Roback Morse, *Forbes*, April 19, 1999.

In 1993, the Senate deemed it quite the nation's business to look into charges against Sen. Bob Packwood—ah, a Republican—some of which were older than Juanita Broaddrick's (they went back to 1969) and none anywhere near as severe. Under pressure of outraged feminists and agitated Democrats, Packwood was forced to resign and Washington pronounced itself satisfied at his political decapitation.

This time around, the move-on Democrats throw up their hands with it's just "he said, she said." (Actually, it is "she said, his lawyer said." He's said nothing.) Do these people have no shame? Of course they don't. But more important, and the reason the feminist cause is irretrievably damaged, is that its erstwhile champions have no arguments. What do they say the next time a public man is charged with grossly exploitative (if consensual) workplace sex? With creating a hostile work environment? With lying under oath in a sexual harassment suit? Good God, with rape?

Let's move on?

| *"The media and pop-culture purveyors stamped the label of sex-phobic on feminists, then condemned them for not living up to the stigma."*

Feminism Has Not Abandoned Its Original Principles

Susan Faludi

Feminist scholar Susan Faludi is the author of *Backlash: The Undeclared War Against American Women* and *Stiffed: The Betrayal of the American Man*. In the following viewpoint, she responds to charges that feminists have betrayed their principles by failing to denounce President Bill Clinton for engaging in sexual acts with former White House intern Monica Lewinsky. In truth, Faludi asserts, feminism has never called for the legal restriction of private acts between two consenting people; the expectation that feminists should condemn adultery and other forms of private sexual behavior stems from the feminist movement's erroneous reputation as "sexphobic"—a reputation created by media pundits.

As you read, consider the following questions:

1. What is the stigma of being a feminist, as described by Faludi?
2. According to the author, what was "feminists' sin" in relation to the Monica Lewinsky scandal?
3. In the author's opinion, what motivates girls to "take their shirts off"?

As the Clinton sex scandal winds to its bitter end, the real scandal is not what did or didn't happen in the corridors of the Oval Office but how it's been used to justify a lot of political foolishness. Witness the latest misrepresentation of feminism.

When I was in college in the late seventies, the primary drawback to declaring oneself a feminist was the stigma that came with it at the time: prude. Why exactly that was the case, after a decade of second-wave feminists celebrating sexual freedom and admiring their vaginas via speculum, was something of a mystery to me. As a young woman with no interest in convent living, I found this aspect of the feminist label irritating. But I quickly learned that it was no more than that, an irritant—and only in theory. In the practice of everyday life, actual young men dealing with actual young women just as quickly came to the obvious, and happy, conclusion that feminist = frigid priss was a spurious equation.

While so many of us grew up personally debunking the myth of the sex-phobic feminist in our own bedrooms, the media clung to that canard the way an exorcist clutches his garlic cloves and crucifix. Anti-feminist press pundits seized every opportunity to decry the women's movement as a band of vice-squad fussbudgets. When Camille Paglia came along to bash feminism for sexual squeamishness, she was instantly granted Most Favoured Media Status. When young author Katie Roiphe railed against campus feminists' supposed fixation on date rape, she was immediately anointed Soundbite Sally. The *New York Times*, in its self-appointed role of Roiphe publicist, stuck her on the cover of the *New York Times Sunday Magazine*, the front of the *New York Times Book Review* and page one of the *New York Times Living* section—though all to little effect. Her actual reading constituency—young women readers—didn't share her shrill perceptions of feminists' supposed sexual hang-ups and her book sales languished.

All predictable fare, I suppose. It's been going on since suffragists were painted prune-faced spinsters. But then emerged, unforeseen, a whole new, inventive way to skewer feminists on the old sex-averse barb.

I first noticed something was up when I got a phone call

from a *Newsweek* reporter back when the biggest White House sex scandal was the antics of President Clinton's adviser Dick Morris, said to be partial to sucking the toes of a prostitute at an old-line Washington hotel. The reporter wanted me to comment on adultery from 'a feminist perspective'. Having bought into the myth that feminists are the puritanical police force of sexual morals, she expected me to express outrage at the spectre of infidelity. When I didn't, she was not only frustrated but a little put out at my failure to perform my designated feminist role: knuckle-rapper of anyone (i.e., any man) whose private behaviour had been deemed socially unacceptable.

When the Monica Lewinsky brouhaha broke, I got another call from a *Newsweek* reporter. This guy was downright surly when I didn't endorse burning Clinton at the stake. He began to shout at me over the phone. What kind of feminist was I, anyway, to 'suddenly' refuse to condemn male sexual behaviour? 'Don't you thing you're being a hypocrite?' he hissed.

The hypocrisy line became instant conventional wisdom. It went like this: feminists embraced Anita Hill when she didn't like Clarence Thomas's sniggering about big-dick porn stars and pubic hairs on Coke cans, but now they are discreetly looking the other way when Clinton is accused of sexual dalliances. Never mind that what feminists were calling for in Hill's case was not suppression of sex but the right of a woman not to have her voice suppressed in a public hearing. Never mind that the women's movement's concerns have always been with the use of sexual harassment to drive women out of the workforce, not with the private acts of two consenting people. Never mind that feminists have never called for the legal or legislative regulation of private sexual behaviour, no matter how repugnant that behaviour may be to one's own personal morality.

A Reputation as Victorian Avengers

No, now feminists' sin was that we had not lived up to our reputation as Victorian avengers. The epithet that was once used to discredit feminism now became our crowning glory, and it was our sacred duty to uphold it or give up the crown. We had failed our legacy as feminists by failing to adhere to the stereotype that had been invented in the first place to hang us. Feminists now found ourselves in the Alice in Wonderland position of having been found guilty twice for two opposite verdicts on the same charge: first we were sentenced for having committed the crime of prudery, then for having not been prudish enough.

The Feminist Stance on Clinton Reveals Strength, Not Weakness

Defining sexual harassment is complex and contentious, even among feminists. And feminists do make self-interested political calculations. But asserting that support of . . . President [Clinton] is somehow hypocritical places a ridiculous expectation on feminism—that it be a political movement that does not behave politically. Perhaps this expectation betrays lingering traces of the old "republican motherhood" justifications for women's political action—only their superior and "apolitical" morality makes women's participation in the public sphere acceptable. Thus by supporting an adulterer who has served their political interests, feminists are seen to have abandoned their role as moral guardians, and therefore relinquished their right to a political presence.

Few people took notice when conservative advocates of family values enthusiastically supported President Reagan, despite his less than ideal family values record (a messy divorce and estranged, bitter children) and irregular church attendance. When women refuse—in spite of differing opinions on just how grossly Clinton has acted, and legitimate debates about sexual harassment—to allow these differences to overshadow a broad base of consensus on other policy issues, they are revealing not the weakness of the feminist movement, but its strength.

Tara Zahra, *American Prospect*, January/February 1999.

In this through-the-looking-glass realm, any feminist who said 'Wait a sec, that's not what I was saying at all!' was immediately ground into mincemeat in the media's mandibles. When Gloria Steinem wrote a common-sensical column pointing out the differences between consensual sex and the legal definition of sexual harassment on the job, the media firemen rang the four-alarm bells. Her words threatened to burn the whole house of feminism down, the pundits insisted—the same pundits who been trying to burn that house down themselves for the past several decades.

The *New York Times* devoted an entire editorial to deploring Steinem's opinion piece and the supposed 'dangers' her article had unleashed on an unsuspecting female public. Three days later, former *New York Times* executive-editor-cum-columnist Abe Rosenthal foamed hysterically (in both senses of the word) against Steinem in his column. 'We are talking about acts that could terrorise some women, and lead them to horrified flight, even to their death,' he thundered. His evidence: six decades ago, he wrote, his sister Bess had run home after encountering a flasher and had died from pneumonia shortly thereafter.

When I wrote in a small item in the *Nation* that a more likely suspect in Bess's death was poverty—Abe's sister contracted pneumonia after endless germ-filled subway commutes to and from her cruddy low-paid secretarial job—I promptly became the next feminist 'hypocrite' to be upbraided by the media. *Time* magazine, among others, promptly singled out this small piece as proof of my having abandoned feminist rectitude in the quest to 'make excuses for the President'.

Tracing the Supposed Decline of Feminism

As it happened, the whole *Time* piece was an effort to besmirch feminism on the sex question. The cover story, entitled hopefully 'Is Feminism Dead?', illustrated its thesis with a set of pictures that traced the supposed decline of feminism from the bun-and-bonnet suffragist to the self-absorbed and sex-fantasizing TV character Ally McBeal. 'With its days of flat shoes and fiery protest behind it,' *Time* intoned, 'feminism is clearly more attractive to Love now.' This, however, was a bad development, according to *Time*, indicating feminism's detour into a ditz-oid realm of Spice Girls rotating their belly buttons, *Bust* magazine gals confessing their vibrator thrills and writer Elizabeth Wurtzel shedding her shirt for the cover of her book, *Bitch*.

'What a comedown for the movement,' the magazine lamented soulfully, a jeremiad that would had been a tad more believable if *Time* hadn't devoted the last 30 years to kicking feminism in the teeth at every opportunity. There is something awful about feminism being invoked to sell lame CDs, magazines and books. But that's hardly evidence that feminism is dead. If anything, it's evidence that women's craving for independence and voice is so immense that, in the absence of real autonomy and authority, an ersatz feminism manufactured and packaged by commercial interests can make zillions. What *Time* was chronicling wasn't, as it thought, feminism's new exhibitionistic tendencies. It was the commercial culture's—and the triumph of its version of sex, a retouched plastic blow-up doll version, a kind of 'death' that produces money but turns human sexuality into an inanimate transaction.

Women want, as do all human beings, to feel they have an effect on the world, that they are engaged and powerful on the public stage. But at century's end, the crushing force of global consumerism has turned the public stage into a display counter. And under that glass, girls take their shirts off because they sense, rightly, that this is the only likely way to exercise 'power' in such an age. In this new market economy, the object of the gaze becomes, if not free, then at least, for her 30 seconds of fame, rich and celebrated.

Young women only need look to *Time* magazine for confirmation of this modern reality. The magazine offered up Ally McBeal's legs for readers' delectation . . . while at the same time cancelling the contract of their one feminist columnist, Barbara Ehrenreich, whose pieces probing deeply into matters of social injustice and economic inequality proved too . . . well, feminist, for the magazine's censorious tastes.

The Real Hypocrisy

The vanquishing of Barbara Ehrenreich is the real hypocrisy. And also an example of the real repression—the kind that spells actual 'dangers' for women's progress, the kind that could indeed 'terrorise some women', women who will never get to gyrate under the display glass.

First the media and pop-culture purveyors stamped the label of sex-phobic on feminists, then condemned them for not living up to the stigma. Now they unroll the glittery new red carpet of consumerism and invite young women to prance down its length in their underwear . . . then condemn them for accepting the invitation. Which just speaks to the truth of feminism's oldest and deepest message—until you stop dutifully following cultural orders and learn to think for yourself, you'll never be nothing but somebody's girl.

Periodical Bibliography

The following articles have been selected to supplement the diverse views presented in this chapter. Addresses are provided for periodicals not indexed in the *Readers' Guide to Periodical Literature*, the *Alternative Press Index*, the *Social Sciences Index*, or the *Index to Legal Periodicals and Books*.

Peter Beinart	"Hypocrites," *New Republic*, March 30, 1998.
Phyllis Chesler	"Letter to a Young Feminist," *On the Issues*, Fall 1996. Available from 29–28 41st Ave., 12th Floor, Long Island City, NY 11101-3303.
Maureen Dowd	"How to Snag 2,000 Men," *New York Times*, July 2, 1997.
Noemie Emery	"Hillary Clinton and the Crisis of Feminism," *Weekly Standard*, March 9, 1998. Available from 1211 Avenue of the Americas, New York, NY 10036.
Nadya Labi	"Girl Power," *Time*, June 19, 1998.
Marianne Means	"What Is a Feminist?" *Liberal Opinion*, July 6, 1998. Available from PO Box 468, Vinton, IA 52349.
Jennifer Roback Morse	"Is Feminism Finished?" *Forbes*, April 19, 1999.
Jeremy Rabkin	"Bill's Fickle Feminists," *American Spectator*, May 1998.
Phyllis Schlafly	"Feminist Pursuit of Unfair Advantages?" *Washington Times*, February 10, 1996.
George Watson	"The Fading of Feminism," *Chronicles*, May 1995. Available from the Rockford Institute, 928 North Main St., Rockford, IL 61103.

CHAPTER 4

What Should the Goals of Feminism Be?

Chapter Preface

In 1983, the Minneapolis city council passed a civil rights ordinance that applied legal restrictions to the production and distribution of pornography. Feminist activists Andrea Dworkin and Catharine A. MacKinnon, who authored the ordinance, argued that pornography violates the civil rights of women and should be banned because it

> is a systematic practice of exploitation and subordination based on sex that differentially harms and disadvantages women. The harm of pornography includes dehumanization, psychic assault, sexual exploitation, forced sex, forced prostitution, physical injury, and social and sexual terrorism and inferiority presented as entertainment.

Because pornography has been linked to the incidence of rape and sexual assault, contend Dworkin and MacKinnon, it is a form of sex discrimination that must be abolished if women are to achieve equality.

Although the ordinance has had little impact on the pornography industry—in each city where the law has passed, U.S. courts struck it down—it has provoked conflict within the feminist movement. Feminist organizations such as Feminists for Free Expression and Feminists Against Censorship denounce the Dworkin/MacKinnon ordinance and other attempts to restrict pornography, claiming that such attempts are inherently incompatible with feminism because they seek to limit free speech. As Barbara Dority explains, "It is only because of the First Amendment in the United States and its equivalents in other countries that women have been able to speak and write in favor of reproductive freedom and gender equality. History shows that censorship and suppression work directly against feminist goals and are often used to limit women's rights in the name of protection. . . . Censorship and suppression of any kind are in direct conflict with feminist principles of freedom and tolerance."

The debate about whether feminists should work for legal restrictions on pornography reflects the larger controversy over what role the government should play in promoting women's equality. The following chapter addresses this question and others relating to the goals of feminism.

> *"The right to an abortion is so central to a woman's dignity, hope, education, and prospects for independence that it must be a feminist issue."*

Feminists Should Support Abortion Rights

Anne Roiphe

Because the right to control one's body is central to women's dignity and independence, argues Anne Roiphe in the following viewpoint, abortion rights are a crucial feminist issue. Roiphe contends that the pro-life movement, through manipulative advertising campaigns, has created the erroneous impression that, as supporters of abortion rights, feminists are hostile to children. In order to change this impression, she maintains, feminists must emphasize the role of abortion rights in protecting the welfare of children, mothers, and families. Roiphe is the author of *Fruitful: A Real Mother in the Modern World*, from which this viewpoint is excerpted.

As you read, consider the following questions:
1. According to the author, how does the abortion debate reflect America's clashing worldviews?
2. In Roiphe's opinion, how has the feminist movement been out-maneuvered by the pro-life movement?
3. Where should feminists draw the line on the issue of abortion, as stated by Roiphe?

P regnancy at certain times, under certain circumstances, can be a real tragedy. This is an ancient truth and was not created by modern feminism. In the days before society became more open and the double standard ruled, women were stigmatized by pregnancy out of wedlock. The child was a bastard and life of mother and child could truly be ruined. Sexual rules were always being broken, someone was always being shamed. Even for a married woman with other children the conception of another child is not necessarily welcome. This is true for women with financial problems with or without mates, it is true for women who are in the midst of their education or training, it is true for women who simply don't feel ready or able to take on the immense burden of a baby or a child. It is also true for women whose pregnancies have occurred through rape or incest, or with men who have left them alone. The fierceness of the desire to have a child is equally balanced by the necessity of not having a child sometimes, under some circumstances. Abortion is as old as history and existed way before feminism made the woman's ownership of her own body a major issue. Abortion is the face of harsh reality and always has been. Before technology, before sterilization, before contraception, the birth of a child was not always the cause for rejoicing. It still isn't. These days abortion intersects so clearly with feminist goals that it appears to be a feminist wish, to abort the fetus, or so the enemies of abortion and feminism would have us think.

Abortion has become a symbolic public issue. The desire to keep women dependent and at home, to hold on to something sacred in a world that tends to strip everything down to its commercial use, to prevent the casual sexual encounter out of puritan sensibility, fear of sexual disorder (which is usually a fear of one's own sexual impulses raging out of control), fear of a world in which life and death are not just God's domain—these are matters that inform the abortion battles.

Clashing Worldviews

Abortion has become the issue that divides the fundamentally religious from the anti-traditional, those who seek personal freedom from those who seek obedience to the decreed ways. Shame, since the upheaval of the nineteen seventies, is no longer a player in the discussion, although certain conservatives would like to control sexual behavior with that old splintered billy club. Now the fight in America is between clashing worldviews, oppositions that can barely coexist. The abortion issue signals an ongoing if unrecognized civil war that may yet lead to our undoing as a civil nation. What presents itself here as a feminist issue of control over one's own body is in fact entangled in questions of ambiguity, contrasting visions of freedom that belong to the religious wars of history. It's amazing that so little blood has been shed so far.

The right to an abortion is so central to a woman's dignity, hope, education, and prospects for independence that it must be a feminist issue. When motherhood is an imposition not a choice, a tragedy not a desire, then women are reduced to their biology, and life with its accumulated disappointments becomes a prison: depression where joy should be. On the other hand, when feminists fight for legal abortion they appear to be fighting against the child that will come. They do in fact appear to be more interested in preventing motherhood than in making life better for the new mothers and children that continually spill across the country, uncountable like the stars in the Milky Way. This matter of image has serious political consequences. To be pro-child is in fact to be pro-choice, to be pro-choice is to be pro-child, but it is easy to make that appear untrue. Every child a wanted child is a less dramatic slogan, less visual, heart-tugging, morally unambiguous, than Save the baby, Life, a beautiful choice, or Child murderer. The feminist movement has allowed itself to be out-maneuvered, out-sloganed, by the rigid right who claim to love children more than the rest of us. It's a false claim, it's a sleight of hand, but it hurts. We have not made the case that every child must be a wanted child strongly enough because that would involve an open public expression of women's love for children which to some feminists seems like stoking the reactionary fires. We don't want to make such a fuss over the wonder of babies that someone might suggest we should go back into the nursery and stay there. Calling for legal abortion is a more attractive position for women so newly liberated from exclusive child care than carrying on about the beautiful choice of a wanted child.

The Power of Pro-Life Rhetoric

The pro-life movement takes out TV ads in which adorable children emerge from behind a school door, they share a sandwich, they sit on the swings, they jump rope, they smile shyly at the camera, and the voice-over says, "Life, what a beautiful choice." The ad speaks in terms so blatantly sentimental that it's hard to resist. We can despise their cleaned-up view of the unwanted child, the way they leave out the bruises of abuse, the effects of poverty, but we can't help but be touched by the living blush of real children at the beginning of their lives. They got us. They got us because our position appears like a negative, a reverse of their image, our position is a graveyard, a collection of fetuses in a jar, stillness in place of movement.

Reprinted with permission of Kirk Anderson.

When we debated abortion back in the prelegal days, we discussed the beginning of life, when was it exactly, and we held hard to the line that life was about breathing air, working lungs, fetal viability. Life could only be extrauterine we said. That was our story. This was philosophically interesting but actually meaningless. The real line between the life that would be if left alone and the life that wasn't because it

143

wasn't left alone is clearly more ambiguous than we would have liked. The advent of sonograms, the earlier age of fetal survival, the knowledge that every pregnant woman has, even in the first days after she discovers that she is pregnant, certainly when the baby kicks within her, that life is really there, means that our position was intellectually weak, more wish than reality. However, their position was no better, simple but not necessarily moral. We drew our line on the absolute question: Is or isn't the embryo alive? We should have drawn the line on whether the fetus was or was not wanted and shaped the debate on that issue instead of getting mired in metaphysics or theology about the beginning of life.

Beginning a New Debate

In some circumstances life is not sacred. To say this is to end the old debate and begin a new one on which we are on firmer ground. To say this is not to instigate massacres or social mayhem. We have always had those, and not because a nation or a tribe allowed legal abortion. To be able to take a shading on the moral chart, to declare that you can't kill a fifteen-month-old child but you can a six-week-old fetus is to accept ambiguity, complications, things that are not black and white but private, morally sticky, sometimes necessary. Every woman who has been pregnant knows that the life within her is life whether she chooses to end it or not. Just as the two-year-old will likely become twenty, so the undisturbed fetus will likely become one. To kill a fetus, however, is not the same as to kill a baby and everyone knows that. To kill a baby without a brain is not the same as to kill a baby with a club foot and everyone knows that too. Life is sacred but sometimes the sacred thing to do is to end life. It is true we stand on a slippery slope but reality and morality are formed and lived on slippery slopes. To be able to make difficult decisions that are not based on immutable rules is a sign of human complexity and indicates a capacity for moral thought as opposed to sheer obedience.

The morality of abortion lies in our capacity to make distinctions of quality, to balance one good against another, one evil against another. The moral outrage of the pro-lifers would be blunted if we made the argument that civilized people can hold the line against murder while acknowledging that sometimes life is not a necessary outcome of its earliest beginning.

The women's movement would be better able to fight off the pro-life forces if we had expressed a deeper concern for children, for family, for the sacrifices that children require of a parent, of a society. If the issue is women's freedom alone it becomes suspect. If the desire for the legalization of abortion is prompted by concern for the welfare of children, of mothers, of families, then we can go on the moral offensive, not just when they try to shoot our doctors but the rest of the time as well.

"As feminists, we must not continue to buy into the historically male world view: that the solution to sociological problems . . . is convenient violence."

Feminists Should Oppose Abortion

Maureen Jones-Ryan

In the subsequent viewpoint, Maureen Jones-Ryan, a member of the antiabortion organization Feminists for Life, asserts that the pro-life position affirms one of the basic tenets of feminism: the belief that every person is deserving of opportunity and respect. If feminists are to promote a more socially responsible world, she argues, they must condemn the violence of abortion and search for alternative solutions to the problems of poverty, overpopulation, and sexual irresponsibility.

As you read, consider the following questions:
1. How does peer pressure influence feminists' positions on abortion, as explained by Jones-Ryan?
2. What alternatives to abortion are cited by the author?
3. According to Jones-Ryan, how do feminists serve as "effective marketing tools"?

Reprinted with permission from "Pro-Life, Pro-Feminism," by Maureen Jones-Ryan, *SisterLife*, April, 3, 1997. Article available at www.serve.com/fem4life/tafarts/jonesrya.htm.

"**F**eminists for Life" is not an oxymoron, it's a redundancy. The reduplicative nature of the phrase is evident in the basic tenets of feminism: that every human being deserves the opportunity to develop into the best she or he is capable of; and that each individual be respected, however minimal or great their development may be.

As a third generation anti-abortion feminist activist, I was raised to work along with my sister and brother feminists in promoting a more socially responsible world, a civilized world that repudiates injustice and violence.

Leo Tolstoy, the Russian novelist and social theoretician who profoundly inspired the developing philosophies of non-violence promoted and lived by Mahatma Gandhi and The Rev. Dr. Martin Luther King, Jr., stated in his diary of 1852, "It is true that slavery is an evil, but an extremely convenient evil."

Justifying Evil Based on Convenience

Pro-abortionists unwittingly have chosen to justify an evil based on convenience rather than struggle honestly and intellectually with the philosophical, sociological, and historical aspects of this momentous life-and-death issue.

It is much more convenient to deny our individual and community responsibilities for social order and the development of a civilized (i.e. non-violent) human condition than to tackle head-on the challenges of preventing unwanted pregnancies.

Through Tolstoy, Gandhi, and King, we are better able to understand the evil inherent in any form of violence. The violence of abortion is indisputable.

The philosophies of these three feminists help us perceive that the practice of non-violence, inconvenient as it may be, can transcend political and cultural boundaries and bring forth visionary, creative solutions to the most complex of problems, including the problem of unwanted pregnancies.

As an anti-abortion feminist activist, I am an enigma to many: to the women's right activists who assume a pro-abortion position is a prerequisite for feminism; and to the right-to-lifers who equate feminism with abortion on demand. Seeing their neat, albeit specious, categories breached is disquieting, inconvenient. Labels and categories enslave the mind and dampen intellectual curiosity, but they certainly are convenient.

Succumbing to Peer Pressure

So many would-be feminists, women who truly seek liberation, freedom, and justice, abandon individualism while succumbing to peer group pressure. Independent research, free thinking and critical analysis succumb to the comfort and security of conformity. The male oppression they so diligently worked to eradicate is replaced, obsequiously, by oppressive dominant groups. (As a member of the Phoenix Chapter of the National Organization for Women, I've not been "officially" requested to relinquish my membership, despite former national president Molly Yard's unenlightened stand against feminists making independent decisions free of dominant group oppression. Ohio NOW forced Pat Goltz to give up her NOW membership, and she went on to co-found Feminists for Life in 1972.) Intellectually responsible feminists choose not to consult a laundry list of any group's position to know what to think and what to say.

Abortion Frees Men, Not Women

Men, not women, are the ones freed by abortion-on-demand. Abortion frees a man from any responsibilities to the child he sires. Abortion cuts the cords of duty and commitment to the child's mother. A few hundred bucks and— "poof!"—problem solved. It's so convenient for men. They don't suffer the terrible medical risks. They don't suffer post-abortion emotional trauma to the degree that women do. But if a woman decides to keep her baby, the baby becomes her problem. Her "right" to abort becomes pressure, even coercion, to do so. . . .

Abortion denigrates the special gift and power specific to women while excusing the worst male tendencies toward immaturity and self-indulgence. Feminism's expansion of sexual libertinism is not so much a victory for women as a capitulation to the lowest impulses of immature and selfish men. The feminist ethos, with abortion at its core, is the secret dream of the irresponsible adolescent boy.

Steve Schwalm, Family Research Council, January 21, 1998.

Many early feminists evolved toward their understanding of the need to work to establish equal rights for women through their attempt to establish basic human rights. Sarah and Angelina Grimke, the first women to attempt to speak out publicly against slavery, soon learned they, as white women, were also slaves being denied even their right to free speech. Elizabeth Cady Stanton and Lucretia Mott came to the brutal understanding of their own inequality when, solely based on gender, they were prevented from speaking at a World Anti-Slavery convention in London, despite being U.S. delegates. Feminists have always spoken out against racial injustice. Why do so many now remain silent when the iniquitous relationship between racialism and pro-abortion legislation is errantly unabashed?

The "Easy" Solution

It is certainly easier for the white, male-dominated state legislatures and Congress to approve (i.e. encourage?) the elimination of the inconvenient fetuses of poor women (i.e. women of color) than it is to work toward a) eliminating poverty; b) increasing education standards for the poor; c) increasing employment opportunities for the poor; d) providing daycare for the working poor; e) funding serious research for improved contraception; and f) developing a long-range plan to build a society that will provide adequate food, housing, and education for all.

It is certainly easier for individual, even feminist, women to support such legislation than to insist each woman take control of the responsibility for her own reproduction and conception prevention. History has proved that we cannot depend on others to take responsibility for our conception decisions.

As feminists, we must not continue to buy into the historically male world view: that the solution to sociological problems (e.g., poverty, overpopulation, individual's sexual irresponsibility) is convenient violence—suffered predominantly by the world's poor.

Historically, feminists have valued human need above the non-feminist world view of "maximization of profits." Abortion is big business, bringing handsome profits to the usual few: white, middle-class, educated. The vociferous, well-meaning, but misguided, feminists who promote abortion serve as effective marketing tools for those businesses making money from the agony of the poor.

Our thesis bears repeating: "Feminists for Life" is not an oxymoron, it's a redundancy.

"Repeated exposure to pornography . . . increased men's trivialization of rape . . . and increased their estimate of the likelihood that they would rape a woman if they could get away with it."

Feminists Should Work to Restrict Pornography

Diana Russell, interviewed by Ann E. Menasche

In the subsequent viewpoint, feminist and civil rights attorney Ann E. Menasche speaks with Diana Russell, a feminist activist, scholar, and the author of several books about violence against women. Russell contends that pornography—defined as material that endorses the sexual degradation of women—is a significant cause of sexual violence. According to Russell, research shows that pornography provokes some men to have rape fantasies and undermines the inhibitions of men who already have the desire to rape. She maintains that feminists must recognize pornography as a form of discrimination against women and educate the public about the harm pornography does to women's lives.

As you read, consider the following questions:

1. According to Russell, how prevalent is violence against women?
2. As explained by the author, what is the major argument against pornography offered by feminists Dworkin and MacKinnon?
3. What steps can feminist activists take to fight pornography, as stated by Russell?

Excerpted with permission from "Violence, Pornography, and Women-Hating," by Diana Russell, interviewed by Ann E. Menasche, *Against the Current*, 1997.

A. M.: How prevalent is violence against women?
D.R.: It's epidemic. In my probability sample that was done in San Francisco in 1978, of 930 women that were interviewed, 44% had been victims of rape or attempted rape sometime in their lives.

That's using a very conservative definition of rape: forced penile-vaginal intercourse, intercourse achieved by threats of violence, and intercourse when the woman was completely physically helpless, for example, unconscious, drugged or asleep, and attempts at such acts. It didn't include forced oral or anal intercourse. Nor did it include statutory rape where there was no force.

For child sexual abuse, the figure was 38%. This percentage excludes exhibitionism, and other non-contact experiences of sexual abuse or harassment. For incest experiences alone, the prevalence figure was 16% and for father-daughter incest it was 4.5%. . . .

Defining Pornography

A.M.: Your book, *Against Pornography*, attempts to establish a link between pornography and violence against women. How do you define pornography?

D.R.: I define pornography as material that combines sex and/or the exposure of genitals with abuse or degradation in a manner that appears to endorse, condone or encourage such behavior. I conceptualize pornography as both a form of hate speech and as discrimination against women.

A.M.: Can you give some examples of what you consider pornographic?

D.R.: Some examples from *Hustler*: a cartoon showing a jackhammer inserted into a woman's vagina with a caption referring to this as "a cure for frigidity." Or of a woman being ground up in a meat grinder. Photos and descriptions of a woman being gang raped on a pool table, described as an erotic turn-on for the woman.

A cartoon of a husband dumping his wife in a garbage can with her naked buttocks sticking out from the can. A cartoon of a father with a tongue in his daughter's ear and his hands in her pants, again as an erotic turn-on. Or of a boss having sex with his secretary while beckoning his colleagues to come into the room to have sex with her also, with the caption referring to this as her "Christmas bonus."

Pictures of dead, decapitated women with amputated bodies, as well as severed nipples and clitorises. In each of these examples, Larry Flynt jokes about rape, battery, sexual harassment, incest, torture, mutilation and death, and presents this violence as sexy.

A.M.: How do you feel about erotica?

D.R.: I define erotica as sexually suggestive or arousing material that is free of sexism, racism, and homophobia, and respectful of all human beings and animals portrayed.

I find nothing degrading about explicit portrayals of sex per se, though erotica can of course be much broader than that. Even the peeling of an orange can be filmed to make it erotic.

A.M.: How do you respond to people who point out that it is impossible to obtain a consensus on what is pornography versus what is erotica, that "one person's erotica is another person's pornography?"

D.R.: There is no consensus on the definitions of many phenomena. Rape is one example. Legal definitions of rape vary considerably in different states. Similarly, millions of court cases have revolved around arguments as to whether a killing constitutes murder or manslaughter. Lack of consensus should not automatically mean that pornography cannot be subject to opprobrium or legal restraint, or that we cannot examine its effects.

Pornography as a Cause of Rape

A.M.: You state in *Against Pornography* that pornography is one of multiple causes of men raping women, other causes being male sex role socialization, sexual abuse in childhood and peer pressure. Could you give a few examples of the research that supports the view that pornography plays a role in causing sexual violence?

D.R.: First, there is the experiment by [Neil] Malamuth in which he shows that being exposed to some typical violent pornography will change those men who weren't force-oriented to begin with into having rape fantasies that they didn't previously have.

Second, there is the research that shows that pornography

undermines the inhibitions of those who already have some desire to rape. For example, the work of [Dolf] Zillmann and [Jennings] Bryant shows that repeated exposure to pornography for a four-week period increased men's trivialization of rape, increased their callousness towards women, made them more likely to say that rape was the responsibility of the victim and that it was not a serious offense, and increased their estimate of the likelihood that they would rape a woman if they could get away with it.

Eroticizing Male Dominance

Regardless of the actual plots of pornographic books, films, or shows, or the representational content of pornographic images, the focal point and purpose of heterosexual pornographic practice is male sexual pleasure. Even when women's pleasure is of issue, it is found in the satisfaction of men's desires, in doing anything and everything that men want or order to be done. Women are objectified and subordinated in the attainment of men's ends. At the center of pornography is an eroticization of male dominance.

Consider the repeated images in pornography of the woman spread-eagled, stalked, bound, beaten, mutilated, gagged, or raped, and of the woman accepting such treatment, and (often) being sexually aroused by it. Even in soft-core and less graphically violent pornography, the subordination of women to men is a unifying theme, expressed through women's sexual servitude, their roles as sexual toys and playthings of men, objects of access and use, whose purpose is to serve men sexually. As [Catharine A.] MacKinnon writes, in pornography,

> Subjection itself, with self-determination ecstatically relinquished, is the content of women's sexual desire and desirability. Women are there to be violated and possessed, men to violate and possess us. . . . On a simple descriptive level, the inequality of hierarchy, of which gender is the primary one, seems necessary for sexual arousal to work. . . . What pornography does goes beyond its content: it eroticizes hierarchy, it sexualizes inequality.

Alisa L. Carse, *Hypatia*, Winter 1995.

Perhaps most important of all is James Check's work making comparisons between the effect on men viewing violent pornography, degrading pornography and erotica in an experimental situation.

Check found that the violent material had the most negative effect, the degrading material had the next most negative effects, and the other sexual material had no negative effects at all. The negative effects he documented included an increase in the self-reported likelihood that the men would actually act out a rape.

"Real Life Harm to Women"

A.M.: Katha Pollitt, writing in the February 2 issue of *The Nation* disputed that pornography caused real life harm to women. Pollitt wrote, "any serious discussion of texts that cause real life harm to women would have to begin with the Bible and the Koran: It isn't porn that drives zealots to fire-bomb abortion clinics or slit the throats of Algerian schoolgirls." How would you respond to that?

D.R.: Nonsense! None of us are claiming that pornography is the single cause of violence in the world. Also, Pollitt's not even using sexual violence as examples. If Pollitt had looked at my book, *Against Pornography*, and studied the examples of pornography and the research reviewed there, I don't think she could continue to take such a position.

A.M.: How do you respond to the charge that the Andrea Dworkin–Catharine MacKinnon approach to fighting pornography amounts to censorship that would dangerously restrict free speech?

D.R.: Dworkin and MacKinnon do not advocate banning or censorship of pornography. What they advocate is that anyone who has been victimized by pornography and can prove it in a court of law should be able to do so. That's not censorship, that's accountability.

Pornography as a Form of Discrimination Against Women

It seems that if you make any proposal against pornography, people equate it with censorship. One of MacKinnon and Dworkin's major contributions in this area is to try to recast the debate about pornography—they maintain that this is not primarily a debate about freedom of speech. It's an issue of discrimination against women.

Discrimination based on sex, race, or sexual orientation is not acceptable and, in some instances, it's illegal. Take sexual harassment, for example. There's a law against sexual harassment, that it constitutes discrimination against women and some men.

Catharine MacKinnon is largely responsible for developing this analysis. She conceptualized sexual harassment in this way. Most people don't protest that the laws against sexual harassment constitute an attack on free speech, that men in the workplace should be able to say whatever they like to women, to proposition them and talk about their breasts, and ask them about their genitals and whatever, as an exercise of their freedom of speech.

It is recognized that such behavior, even though it involves speech, is not acceptable, that it's discrimination and it's abuse of power and it makes a hostile environment against women. Even the display of pornography in the workplace is considered to contribute to a hostile environment and is therefore against the law.

We are making a similar argument, that pornography outside the workplace also makes for a hostile environment, a dangerous environment because it promotes rape and other forms of sexual violence.

A.M.: Given that this controversy exists, do you think it is helpful to discuss what one thinks about pornography separately from one's position on what should be done about it?

D.R.: Yes, I think it's imperative! I try to insist that people not start discussing what to do about it before they've discussed if it is damaging or not. If it's not damaging, you don't have to do anything about it.

There are people who take the position that pornography is extremely damaging, but the law isn't the way to handle it. Nikki Craft is one feminist and dedicated activist who takes this stance.

Organizing Against Pornography

A.M.: Could you mention some of the ways that a person can organize against pornography if one is opposed to censorship and disagrees with the Dworkin-MacKinnon approach?

D.R.: In my book *Making Violence Sexy*, I have a whole section at the end about feminist actions against pornography, none of which constitute censorship or requires the passage of any laws. You can do educational campaigns like the recent campaign against the movie, "The People vs. Larry Flynt." We organized press conferences and picket-lines. We were not advocating censorship. We were not even advocating boycotting the movie, although boycotts do not constitute censorship either. Somehow, whenever we express our own First Amendment rights to protest pornography, we're called censors—which is absurd.

I think education is important because half the people who say pornography is fine don't have a clue what they're really talking about. Again and again, we find if you show people what's in pornography, they are shocked, particularly women.

A.M.: What was the objective of your campaign against the Larry Flynt movie?

D.R.: Our objective was to educate people about the lies that are told in the movie, to point out the violent and women-hating content of *Hustler* magazine that was completely omitted from the film, and to point out what Larry Flynt is really like, so Milos Foreman and Oliver Stone's efforts to turn him into a hero will be undermined.

Flynt himself has said that the film is a massive free advertising campaign for *Hustler* magazine. Since the movie, the circulation of *Hustler* has gone up, in spite of the fact that the movie has not done so well at the box office. I believe it only made about twenty million whereas it cost about sixty million to make. It was expected to be a great success, but this was before feminists began protesting. . . .

Increasing Consciousness About Male Violence Against Women

A.M.: How can change come about for women? How can we create a world where women are not kept in our places by violence and the threat of violence?

D.R.: We need to increase the level of consciousness about male violence against women. We've made some progress in the United States in many areas. For example, sexual harassment is now recognized, it wasn't recognized before. . . .

The old way of men blaming women for the violence has

been challenged by feminists. However, we haven't yet seen a decline in the violence itself.

I often think we would be more effective if women as a gender were more militant in our response. I'm not talking about on an individual level—although I favor that too. But we must join together in organizations to act more militantly, even if those organizations are small four-women ones.

As with pornography, those who are the victims of it, the targets—as Black people are with racist material—really have to be the mobilizers. I think direct action and civil disobedience would be extremely effective for women to use.

We are just a handful of people trying to educate a nation, meanwhile, pornography is a multibillion dollar industry miseducating people. Though many women have been arrested for peace and civil rights work, very few women appear to be willing to get arrested for feminist causes.

People talk about a war between the sexes, but it's more like a massacre, because women often don't fight back. And we can't all fight our separate battles in our own homes.

Organizing together is really the secret; organization is the answer to making change. As Andrea Dworkin has said, women have been very good at "endurance" but not at "resistance." We must change this.

"Pornography benefits women, both personally and politically."

Feminists Should Work to Protect Pornography

Wendy McElroy

In the viewpoint that follows, Wendy McElroy, author of *XXX: A Woman's Right to Pornography*, contends that the traditional feminist position on pornography—the belief that pornography commodifies and exploits women—is fallacious. In reality, argues McElroy, pornography benefits women on a personal level by broadening their knowledge of sex, and on a political level by strengthening their right to free speech.

As you read, consider the following questions:

1. As stated by McElroy, what specific accusations are aimed at pornography?
2. According to the author, what are the four ways in which pornography benefits women personally?
3. What are the four ways in which pornography benefits women politically, as expressed by the author?

Excerpted with permission from "A Feminist Overview of Pornography, Ending in a Defense Thereof," by Wendy McElroy, *Free Inquiry*. Article available at www.zetetics.com/mac/freeinq.htm.

"**P**ornography benefits women, both personally and politically." This sentence opens my book *XXX: A Woman's Right to Pornography*, and it constitutes a more extreme defense of pornography than most feminists are comfortable with. I arrive at this position after years of interviewing hundreds of sex workers. . . .

The most common [feminist position on pornography]—at least, in academia—is that pornography is an expression of male culture through which women are commodified and exploited. . . .

The specific accusations hurled at pornography include:
1. Pornography degrades women.
2. Pornography leads directly to violence against women.
3. Pornography is violence against women, in that:
    a. women are physically coerced into pornography;
    b. women involved in the production of pornography are so psychologically damaged by patriarchy that they are incapable of giving informed or 'real' consent.

A Critique of Anti-Porn Feminism

Do these accusations stand up under examination?
Pornography Is Degrading to Women.
'Degrading' is a subjective term. I find commercials in which women become orgasmic over soapsuds to be tremendously degrading. The bottom line is that every woman has the right to define what is degrading and liberating for herself.

The assumed degradation is often linked to the 'objectification' of women: that is, porn converts them into sexual objects. What does this mean? If taken literally, it means nothing because objects don't have sexuality; only beings do. But to say that porn portrays women as 'sexual beings' makes for poor rhetoric. Usually, the term 'sex objects' means showing women as 'body parts', reducing them to physical objects. What is wrong with this? Women are as much their bodies as they are their minds or souls. No one gets upset if you present women as 'brains' or as 'spiritual beings'. If I concentrated on a woman's sense of humor to the exclusion of her other characteristics, is this degrading? Why is it degrading to focus on her sexuality?

Pornography Leads to Violence Against Women.
A cause-and-effect relationship is drawn between men viewing pornography and men attacking women, especially in the form of rape. But studies and experts disagree as to whether any relationship exists between pornography and violence, between images and behavior. Even the pro-censorship Meese Commission Report admitted that the data connecting pornography to violence was unreliable.

Other studies, such as the one prepared by feminist Thelma McCormick (1983) for the Metropolitan Toronto Task Force on Violence Against Women, find no pattern to connect porn and sex crimes. Incredibly, the Task Force suppressed the study and reassigned the project to a pro-censorship male, who returned the 'correct' results. His study was published.

What of real world feedback? In Japan, where pornography depicting graphic and brutal violence is widely available, rape is much lower per capita than in the United States, where violence in porn is severely restricted.

Pornography Is Violence.
Women Are Coerced into Pornography:
Not one woman of the dozens of women in porn with whom I spoke reported being coerced. Not one knew of a woman who had been. Nevertheless, I do not dismiss reports of violence: every industry has its abuses. And anyone who uses force or threats to make a woman perform should be charged with kidnapping, assault, and/or rape. Any pictures or film should be confiscated and burned, because no one has the right to benefit from the proceeds of a crime.

Women Who Pose for Porn Are so Traumatized by Patriarchy They Cannot Give Real Consent:
Although women in pornography appear to be willing, anti-porn feminists know that no psychologically healthy woman would agree to the degradation of pornography. Therefore, if agreement seems to be present, it is because the women have 'fallen in love with their own oppression' and must be rescued from themselves.

A common emotional theme in the porn actresses I have interviewed is a love of exhibitionism. Yet if such a woman declares her enjoyment in flaunting her body, anti-porn feminists claim she is not merely a unique human being who reacts from a different background or personality. She is psychologically damaged and no longer responsible for her actions. In essence, this is a denial of a woman's right to choose anything outside the narrow corridor of choices offered by political/sexual correctness. The right to choose hinges on the right to make a 'wrong' choice, just as freedom of religion entails the right to be an atheist. After all, no one will prevent a woman from doing what they think she should do.

A Pro-Sex Defense of Pornography

As a 'pro-sex' feminist, I contend: Pornography benefits women, both personally and politically. It benefits them personally in several ways:

1. It provides sexual information on at least three levels:
    a. it gives a panoramic view of the world's sexual possibilities. This is true even of basic sexual information such as masturbation, which seems to come less naturally to women than to men. It is not uncommon for women to reach adulthood without knowing how to give themselves pleasure.
    b. it allows women to 'safely' experience sexual alternatives and satisfy a healthy sexual curiosity. The world is a dangerous place. By contrast, pornography can be a source of solitary enlightenment. Pornography allows women to experiment in the privacy of their own bedrooms, on a television set that can be turned off whenever she has had enough.
    c. it provides a different form of information than textbooks or discussion. It offers the emotional information that comes only from experiencing something either directly or vicariously. It provides us with a sense how it would 'feel' to do something.

2. Pornography strips away the emotional confusion that so often surrounds real world sex. Pornography allows women to enjoy scenes and situations that would be anathema to them in real life. Take, for example, one of the most common fantasies reported by women—the fantasy of 'being taken', of being raped. The first thing to understand is that a rape fantasy does not represent a desire for the real

thing. It is a fantasy. The woman is in control of the smallest detail of every act.

The Victim Mentality of Anti-Porn Activists

Both [Andrea] Dworkin and [Catharine A.] MacKinnon have . . . argued that women who participate in or enjoy pornography or have heterosexual sex are brainwashed or programmed into these activities by men. In order to maintain this view they have to virtually obliterate the idea that women are active agents in the choices they make about their lives and their sexual activity. Dworkin and MacKinnon instead reinforce the idea of women as victims, as passive and helpless, needing to be guided into an understanding of the "errors of their ways" by those who "truly" understand the nature of sexuality.

This amounts to prescribing a "politically correct" sex and an elitist view of social change—of how women should fight against their oppression. Instead of being encouraged to challenge, experiment and fight against the ways they are oppressed, thus empowering themselves and building up the collective strength of the movement through the process of struggle, women are told to rely on a new set of "feminist" experts.

This is an old and very sad story for women. It is exactly what the right-wing moralists proclaim to keep women in their traditional dependent roles of wives and mothers. As Jane Campbell has said, "it is akin to a new brand of moralism which can too easily result in divisions between good feminists and bad (or at least ignorant) women. It is a reversal of the feminist commitment in sexual politics of asserting women's active and independent sexual needs, whether they be with men or women."

Emma Webb, *Pornography and Censorship: Silence or Choice?*, 1995.

Why would a healthy woman daydream about being raped? There are dozens of reasons. Perhaps by losing control, she also sheds all sense of responsibility for and guilt over sex. Perhaps it is the exact opposite of the polite, gentle sex she has now. Perhaps it is flattering to imagine a particular man being so overwhelmed by her that he must have her. Perhaps she is curious. Perhaps she has some masochistic feelings that are vented through the fantasy. Is it better to bottle them up?

Breaking Cultural and Political Stereotypes

3. Pornography breaks cultural and political stereotypes, so that each woman can interpret sex for herself. Anti-feminists tell women to be ashamed of their appetites and urges. Pornography tells them to accept and enjoy them. Pornography provides reassurance and eliminates shame. It says to women 'you are not alone in your fantasies and deepest darkest desires. Right there, on the screen are others who feel the same urges and are so confident that they flaunt them.'

4. Pornography can be good therapy. Pornography provides a sexual outlet for those who—for whatever reason—have no sexual partner. Perhaps they are away from home, recently widowed, isolated because of infirmity. Perhaps they simply choose to be alone. Sometimes, masturbation and vicarious sex are the only alternatives to celibacy. Couples also use pornography to enhance their relationship. Sometimes they do so on their own, watching videos and exploring their reactions together. Sometimes, the couples go to a sex therapist who advises them to use pornography as a way of opening up communication on sex. By sharing pornography, the couples are able to experience variety in their sex lives without having to commit adultery.

Pornography Benefits Women Politically

Pornography benefits women politically in many ways, including the following:

1. Historically, pornography and feminism have been fellow travelers and natural allies. Both have risen and flourished during the same periods of sexual freedom; both have been attacked by the same political forces, usually conservatives. Laws directed against pornography or obscenity, such as the Comstock Law in the late 1880's, have always been used to hinder women's rights, such as birth control. Although it is not possible to draw a cause-and-effect relationship between the rise of pornography and that of feminism, they both demand the same social conditions—namely, sexual freedom.

2. Pornography is free speech applied to the sexual realm. Freedom of speech is the ally of those who seek change: it is the enemy of those who seek to maintain control. Pornogra-

phy, along with all other forms of sexual heresy, such as homosexuality, should have the same legal protection as political heresy. This protection is especially important to women, whose sexuality has been controlled by censorship through the centuries.

3. Viewing pornography may well have a cathartic effect on men who have violent urges toward women. If this is true, restricting pornography removes a protective barrier between women and abuse.

4. Legitimizing pornography would protect women sex workers, who are stigmatized by our society. Anti-pornography feminists are actually undermining the safety of sex workers when they treat them as 'indoctrinated women'. Dr. Leonore Tiefer, a professor of psychology, observed in her essay "On Censorship and Women":

"These women have appealed to feminists for support, not rejection . . . Sex industry workers, like all women, are striving for economic survival and a decent life, and if feminism means anything it means sisterhood and solidarity with these women."

The law cannot eliminate pornography, any more than it has been able to stamp out prostitution. But making pornography illegal will further alienate and endanger women sex workers.

| "The feminist movement will be most effective if we can unite internationally."

Feminists Should Seek International Rights for Women

Jennie Ruby and Karla Mantilla

In the following viewpoint, Jennie Ruby and Karla Mantilla, writers for the feminist newspaper *Off Our Backs*, contend that the feminist movement must unite across the globe in order to protect the rights of women who are living under regimes dominated by religious fundamentalists. Ruby and Mantilla argue that a global feminist agenda is not, as some claim, an attempt to impose the values of Western societies on other countries. Women from all cultures deserve and want full equality to men and the basic right of self-determination.

As you read, consider the following questions:

1. According to Ruby and Mantilla, why have religious fundamentalists been able to garner so much support?
2. What are the justifications offered for abuses of women in non-Western cultures, as explained by the authors?
3. As the authors state, why is an economic analysis so important to the success of feminist programs?

Reprinted with permission from "Why We Need International Feminism," by Jennie Ruby and Karla Mantilla, *Off Our Backs*, March 1997.

A ll year long we are absorbed in fighting the problems of women in our own country and culture. International Women's Day is an opportunity to look up from our own struggles and see the connections between women's struggles across the world. By reading about the experiences of women in other countries, . . . we can see that the backlash against women is global. Women fighting against Islamic fundamentalists are fighting the same cause as women in the United States facing off with the Christian religious right. The rightwing religious backlash is not a peculiarity of one or two countries. It is global. We need to understand that so we can foster international solidarity with women from across the globe, and so that we can exchange strategies that work.

Most of all, we need to understand why a fundamentalist backlash is happening in so many countries so that we can understand how to combat it in our own. It is not happening simply because a few judgmental, overzealous, wrongheaded, religiously intolerant men have suddenly been able to amass political power out of sheer pigheadedness (although that may play a part). This could explain a religious backlash in one country, but it does not explain why the backlash is occurring in so many countries at once.

Why Us, Why Now?

There are some interesting answers in a wonderful book about international feminism, *Identity Politics and Women*, edited by Valentine M. Moghadam. According to Moghadam, the reason religious fundamentalists have been able to garner so much support is that global capitalism has created a new class of disenfranchised people. The real reason for fundamentalist resurgence is economic inequality.

People who are attracted to and join fundamentalist movements tend not to be well-off or in power (although the movements are often led by or manipulated by those in power). Rather than feeling solidarity with other oppressed people or other disenfranchised groups, they latch onto nationalistic, ethnic, or religious identities to gain a feeling of empowerment. They want to rectify their situation by attempting to restore an often mythical traditional moral order. Unfortunately, this not only does not succeed for them, it further oppresses those with whom they might otherwise have joined forces.

It is not coincidental, for example, that fundamentalist Islam and fundamentalist Christianity both impose restrictions on women. Isn't it interesting that the religious values of keeping women in the home, restricting their movements outside the home, forbidding them birth control, etc., also happen to keep women from competing with men in the workplace?

Western Imperialism?

In many third world countries that are experiencing backlash movements, the ideas of human rights, women's rights, equality, and self-determination are portrayed by those in power as Western or American ideas that do not rightfully apply to other cultures. . . . One of the arguments used against making it illegal to sell one's child into prostitution is that is a Western idea and not appropriate to Thai culture. One of the justifications for the extreme oppression of women in Iran has been that it is authentically Iranian to do so; arguments to the contrary are dismissed as just Western ideas. Female genital mutilation has been justified on the grounds that it is a cultural tradition. The idea that women should not be deprived of their most basic rights has been dubbed "cultural imperialism," so that feminism is billed as an attempt to impose American or Western culture in other countries.

As feminists we need to know this argument is not true. Women from all cultures in the world want to have full equality to men, want to have the right to self-determination, to education, to birth control. These are not Western and certainly not American ideas. The suggestion that they are is merely a ploy on the part of backlash movements. In fact, Americans have their own contingent of people who believe in forcing women back into the home, denying them control over reproduction and economic self-determination. This is happening at a time of great economic uncertainty in the United States, and at a time when the labor movement is at an all time low. In the United States, as elsewhere, the justification for these ideas is cultural and religious tradition.

This is why an economic analysis is so important to the

success of feminist programs. Attempting to stop the religious right without addressing the economic inequalities which cause it to be so attractive to so many people will be fruitless. This is not merely an ideological battle, it is also an economic battle. If we fight for economic justice and equality, we may remove the fuel for their movement.

Because all women bear the brunt of the outdated cultural

The Convention on the Elimination of All Forms of Discrimination Against Women

On 18 December 1979, the Convention on the Elimination of All Forms of Discrimination Against Women was adopted by the United Nations General Assembly. It entered into force as an international treaty on 3 September 1981 after the twentieth country had ratified it. By the tenth anniversary of the Convention in 1989, almost one hundred nations have agreed to be bound by its provisions. . . .

Among the international human rights treaties, the Convention takes an important place in bringing the female half of humanity into the focus of human rights concerns. The spirit of the Convention is rooted in the goals of the United Nations: to reaffirm faith in fundamental human rights, in the dignity and worth of the human person, in the equal rights of men and women. The present document spells out the meaning of equality and how it can be achieved. In so doing, the Convention establishes not only an international bill of rights for women, but also an agenda for action by countries to guarantee the enjoyment of those rights.

In its preamble, the Convention explicitly acknowledges that "extensive discrimination against women continues to exist," and emphasizes that such discrimination "violates the principles of equality of rights and respect for human dignity." Discrimination is understood as "any distinction, exclusion or restriction made on the basis of sex . . . in the political, economic, social, cultural, civil or any other field." The Convention gives positive affirmation to the principle of equality by requiring States' parties to take "all appropriate measures, including legislation, to ensure the full development and advancement of women, for the purpose of guaranteeing them the exercise and enjoyment of human rights and fundamental freedoms on a basis of equality with men."

United Nations, available at www.un.org/womenwatch/daw/cedaw/intro.htm.

systems of patriarchy, we must unite across cultures to sustain and support ourselves and each other. This does not mean that we all have to abandon the richness of our own cultures to do so. But the basic human rights of women need to be provided within all cultures. The feminist movement will be most effective if we can unite internationally. Each of our struggles may be specific to our own culture, but the enemy is not.

> *"[The] claim that radical American feminism is the only permissible standard for women everywhere has resurrected [Rudyard] Kipling's 'civilizing mission.'"*

Feminists Should Not Seek International Rights for Women

Paul Craig Roberts

Nationally syndicated columnist Paul Craig Roberts maintains in the subsequent viewpoint that feminists are wrong to pursue an international policy on women's rights. American feminists who want to impose their absolutist standards of gender equality on other countries are self-righteous and ethnocentric, Roberts contends.

As you read, consider the following questions:

1. What comparison does Roberts make between global feminism and communism?
2. What is the nature of the feminist global agenda, as described by the author?
3. What evidence does the author provide that American radical feminists do not occupy the progressive ground?

Reprinted from "Feminist Fog in Foggy Bottom," by Paul Craig Roberts, *The Washington Times*, April 7, 1999. Reprinted with permission from Paul Craig Roberts and Creators Syndicate.

U.S. Secretary of State Madeleine Albright declared last week that "the furtherance of women's rights is a central priority of American foreign policy." This was the same week that Reagan-era defense official Frank Gaffney surveyed the "storm clouds gathering on the horizon" in Iraq, Israel, Russia, China, Bosnia, and Korea and concluded that heavy weather is in store "for U.S. interests around the globe." But the only ominous portent that our secretary of state can divine is "sexism," against which she has declared a world war.

This fatuous elevation of the agenda of radical American feminists to a central priority of U.S. foreign policy is reminiscent of the ideological war communism declared against capitalism, only instead of the capitalist as the villain it is men in general. Nevertheless, "it is our mission," says Mrs. Albright. "It is the right thing to do."

Feminist Ethnocentrism

Mrs. Albright's ethnocentrism would once have brought howls of indignation from liberals, who spent the 20th century insisting we should learn to respect and tolerate other cultures and not believe that our values are superior. Anthropologists such as Margaret Mead, Ruth Benedict and Franz Boas were horrified by the idea Western civilization was somehow superior and had a mission to bring its standards to the rest of the world. Rudyard Kipling's 1899 poem, "The White Man's Burden," which glorified the British mission of civilizing the heathens of the world was a favorite whipping boy of the cultural relativists.

Similarly, Edward B. Tylor's view of civilization as a spectrum from "European nations at one end of the social series and savage tribes at the other" was assailed for the heinous crime of considering one's culture to be morally superior. Ruth Benedict's book, *Patterns of Culture*, published in 1934, declared all standards of behavior to be of equal value and culturally relative. She even praised cannibalism and incest as valid cultural adaptations.

But this was before liberals found their own superior standards to impose on the rest of the world. Once liberal relativism had done its job of destroying traditional Western cultural standards, liberals became more ethnocentric than Kipling. Mrs. Albright intends to force radical feminism down every country's throat, and those who resist are infidels.

The Nature of the Feminist Agenda

The nature of this agenda was made clear at the United Nations, where Mrs. Albright was previously ensconced. Just prior to the U.N.'s 1995 Women's Conference in Beijing (of all places), U.N. official James Gustave Speth bragged to the *Washington Post* about the plan to impose affirmative action policies throughout the world in order "to move forward to establish gender equality." The U.N. instrument designed to codify gender quotas into international law in order to shatter the alleged "global glass ceiling" is known as the U.N. Convention on the Elimination of [All Forms of] Discrimination Against Women. Mrs. Albright is currently wooing Senate Foreign Relations Committee Chairman Jesse Helms in her effort to gain his support for U.S. ratification.

The Arrogance of American Radical Feminists

If only Margaret Mead were here to excoriate Mrs. Albright's self-righteous ethnocentrism, and Ruth Benedict to ask our secretary of state to justify her absolutist views on what is appropriate for women. The liberal scholars of yesterday would have beaten Mrs. Albright to a pulp. How can Mrs. Albright be so arrogant as to claim American radical feminists occupy the progressive ground? Islam condemns American feminism for forcing women to be corrupted in the marketplace and the political arena and by allowing them to dishonor themselves and their parents with sexual promiscuity and perversion. Taboos against adultery have disappeared in the United States, but they remain in force in other cultures. In Afghanistan, adulterers are still stoned.

Mrs. Albright's claim that radical American feminism is the only permissible standard for women everywhere has resurrected Kipling's "civilizing mission." Only this time it is the Feminist Woman's Burden. This new imperialism will make the Middle East, Asia, and Africa even more difficult areas for our foreign policy as we, to paraphrase Kipling, send forth the best we breed in paternalistic care of our new-caught heathen peoples.

"Without a constitutional guarantee of women's equality, . . . favorable rulings and good laws on women's rights can be ignored, revoked or overruled."

Women's Less than Full Equality Under the U.S. Constitution

Patricia Ireland

National Organization for Women president Patricia Ireland claims in the following viewpoint that the equal rights amendment (ERA)—introduced in 1923 by suffragist leader Alice Paul—is an essential part of the effort to secure equality for American women. According to Ireland, historical Supreme Court rulings on women's rights, many of which attempted to "protect" women from making too much money, demonstrates the need for the ERA. A constitutional guarantee of women's equality would ensure that the progress made on women's rights will not be overturned. Ireland is the author of *What Women Want*.

As you read, consider the following questions:

1. How has the constitution excluded women, as explained by Ireland?
2. What examples does the author offer of the Supreme Court's discriminatory rulings in regard to women?
3. As Ireland states, what recent court case proves that inequities still exist in American society?

At a time when women are astronauts and truck drivers, it is hard to believe that the U.S. Constitution does not guarantee women the same rights as men. For most women, equality is a bread-and-butter issue. Women are still paid less on the job and charged more for everything from dry cleaning to insurance. The value of a woman's unpaid work in the home is often not taken into account in determining divorce settlements and pension benefits. When women turn to the courts to right these wrongs, they are at a distinct disadvantage because of what has and hasn't happened to the Constitution.

In 1776 Abigail Adams urged her husband, John, that he and other framers of our founding documents should, "Remember the ladies." John, who went on to become our second president, responded, "Depend upon it. We know better than to repeal our masculine systems," and women were left out of the Constitution.

Nearly a hundred years later, Congress adopted amendments to the Constitution to end slavery and provide justice to former slaves. The 14th Amendment, passed in 1868, guaranteed all "persons" the right to "equal protection under the law." However, the second section of the amendment used the words "male citizens," in describing who would be counted in determining how many representatives each state gets in Congress. This was the first time the Constitution said point blank that women were excluded. Similarly, the 15th Amendment in 1870 extended voting rights to all men—but not to any women.

It wasn't all doom and gloom for women in the 19th and early 20th centuries, though. Two women active in world anti-slavery efforts, Lucretia Mott and Elizabeth Cady Stanton, were leaders at the first-ever "Women's Rights Convention" in Seneca Falls, N.Y., in 1848. Their "Declaration of Sentiments" included this play on the Declaration of Independence, "We hold these truths to be self-evident: that all men and women are created equal."

These women and others went on to form what became known as the suffrage movement. We now consider the suffragists the "first wave" of the U.S. feminist movement. During their long campaign to win women the right to vote, they used strategies including marches, pickets, arrests and hunger strikes. They triumphed in 1920 when the states ratified the 19th Amendment to the Constitution, which corrected the long-time injustice the 15th Amendment had put into writing.

Suffragist leader Alice Paul authored the Equal Rights Amendment (ERA) to remedy women's exclusion from the 14th Amendment. Introduced in 1923, the ERA was buried in Congress for nearly 50 years. In the late 1960s, the "second wave" of feminist activists took up Alice Paul's cause. After getting the ERA voted out of Congress, we held marches, organized boycotts, lobbied and worked on election campaigns to try to get it passed by the necessary three-fourths of the states. When an arbitrary time limit expired in 1982, the ERA was just three states short of the 38 required for ratification.

The history of Supreme Court rulings on women's rights makes clear why a constitutional guarantee of women's equality is needed. During the first 200 years of our country's history, the Supreme Court justices never saw a discriminatory law against women they didn't like. Illinois wanted to keep women from practicing law? The court in 1873 cited "the law of the Creator" as good enough reason to protect these delicate creatures—grown women—from being sullied by the corruption of legal and business practices.

Time and again, women were really being protected from making too much money. Oregon wanted to limit the number of hours women could work? The court in 1908 ruled that women must "rest upon and look to (men) for protection" and also—in a contradictory view of men—that the law was needed "to protect (women) from the greed as well as the passion of man." Michigan wanted to allow women to work as waitresses but keep them out of higher-paid bartender jobs? The court in 1948 did not see this as a violation of the Constitution's guarantee of "equal protection."

In modern times, Supreme Court rulings on women's rights have zigged and zagged, backward and forward. In a 1961 case, the justices upheld Florida's virtual exclusion of women from juries because "women are the center of home and family life." The defendant had bludgeoned her husband to death and wanted jurors who might understand how she could be driven to such a deed.

Finally, in 1971, pioneering feminist attorney Ruth Bader Ginsburg made the first breakthrough in the court's "anything goes" attitude toward sex discrimination. She convinced the court to throw out an Idaho law that automatically gave preference to a man over an equally qualified woman when appointing the person responsible for disposing of the property of someone who has died. Ginsburg went on to become the second woman appointed to serve on the Supreme Court. In 1973, the Court struck down a U.S. Air Force policy that automatically gave a married man family housing and medical allowances, while a married woman had to prove she was the "head of household," i.e., that she provided all of her own expenses plus at least half of her family's in order to qualify for the family benefits.

Why Women Need the ERA

The need for the ERA can be expressed simply as a warning. Unless we put into the Constitution the bedrock principle that equality of rights cannot be denied or abridged on account of sex, the political and judicial victories women have achieved with their blood, sweat, and tears for the past two centuries are vulnerable to erosion or reversal at any time—now or in the future.

Congress has the power to make laws that replace existing laws—and to do so by a simple majority. Therefore, many of the current legal protections against sex discrimination can be removed by the ratio of a 51–49 vote. . . . With an affirmation of equal rights in place constitutionally through the Equal Rights Amendment, progress in eliminating sex discrimination would be much harder to reverse.

Would anyone really want to turn back the clock on women's advancement? Ask the members of Congress who have tried to cripple Title IX, which requires equal opportunity in education—who have opposed the Violence Against Women Act, the Fair Pensions Act, and the Paycheck Fairness Act—who voted to pay for Viagra for servicemen but oppose funding for family planning and contraception—who for over a decade have blocked U.S. ratification of the United Nations Convention on the Elimination of All Forms of Discrimination Against Women (CEDAW).

Roberta W. Francis, Chair, ERA Summit.

But in 1977 the justices were back to an old-fashioned view, a more narrow reading of women's equality. A bright eighth-grade girl, named Susan, who'd won science awards, wanted to attend Philadelphia's all-boys Central High. It was an academically superior public school; even the school board admitted Girls High had inferior science facilities. But the Supreme Court upheld Central High's exclusion of Susan solely because she was a girl.

More recently, in a 1987 decision that is the only Supreme Court case dealing with affirmative action for women, the justices upheld a county's voluntary plan. The justices allowed the promotion to stand, and the woman became the first ever promoted to one of the county's 238 skilled craft jobs. A qualified woman was promoted over a man who had a slightly higher score based on interviews with a team of three men. One of them had called the woman a "rabble rousing skirt" and another had refused to issue her the required coveralls for a previous job.

A case that was before the court in its 1996–1997 term drove home the inequities that still exist at the dawn of the 21st century. A jury had convicted a judge of violating the civil rights of five women by raping, sexually assaulting and harassing the women. An appeals court overruled the jury. Even though courts have ruled repeatedly that it is a violation of a person's civil rights to be beaten by a police officer, the appeals court could not see anything in the Constitution that would put this judge on notice that it is just as wrong to rape a woman.

Without a constitutional guarantee of women's equality, even favorable rulings and good laws on women's rights can be ignored, revoked or overruled. Feminist activists have not given up on a women's equality amendment. We know that to get women into the Constitution we will have to elect a lot more people who support that idea. We look to the young women and men who are addressing issues of equality and justice in high schools across the country. We are confident that this "third wave" will soon be ready to accept the baton.

| *"'Equality' has nothing to do with [the] struggle [of ERA supporters]."*

Women Would Not Benefit from Changes to the U.S. Constitution

Concerned Women for America

In the viewpoint that follows, the Concerned Women for America (CWA), a public policy women's organization that promotes conservative values, criticizes the feminist effort to institute an equal rights amendment (ERA). Although the ERA became null in 1982 because the required number of states had not ratified it, notes the author, feminists continue to promote the ERA against the will of the people. If passed, warns the CWA, an equal rights amendment would provide a legal basis for abortion and homosexual rights, and would affirm the feminist social code that belittles housewives.

As you read, consider the following questions:

1. As explained by the author, why has the ERA failed to take effect?
2. How will the ERA usher in homosexual rights, as asserted by the Concerned Women for America?
3. According to the author, what repressive social codes govern housekeeping?

Excerpted with permission from "The 'Second Wave's' Last Hurrah: Equal Rights Amendment Resurrected," by Concerned Women for America, November 3, 1999, available at www.cwfa.org/library/family/1999-11-03_era.shtml.

The "Equal Rights Amendment"? Didn't that die in 1982? Not quite. Militant feminists are still on the march to garner ratification of this intrusive behemoth. The Equal Rights Amendment (ERA) states:

Section 1: Equality of rights under the law shall not be denied or abridged by the United States or by any state on account of sex.

Section 2: The Congress shall have the power to enforce, by appropriate legislation, the provisions of this article.

Section 3: This amendment shall take effect two years after the date of ratification.

The History of the ERA

Alice Paul of the National Women's Party authored the original ERA in 1923. Introduced as the "Lucretia Mott Amendment"—in honor of the suffragist—it stated: "Men and women shall have equal rights throughout the United States and every place subject to its jurisdiction." Early reformers opposed the amendment, fearing it would undo their hard-earned protective labor laws which treated women differently. In 1943, Paul rewrote the amendment, now called the "Alice Paul Amendment," which is the current version.

Introduced in every session of Congress since 1923, the ERA eventually passed in 1972 and was sent to the states for ratification. Starting with the 18th Amendment, which established the Prohibition in 1917, Congress has placed a seven-year deadline for ratification of constitutional amendments. (The 19th Amendment for women's suffrage was an exception.) The ERA also received a seven-year deadline. Radical feminist groups (the "Second Wave") pushed for ratification. Motivated by them—and the homosexual and abortion rights the ERA would establish—conservative women organized opposition. In fact, the birth of Concerned Women for America in 1979 is rooted in fighting the ERA.

Twenty-two states ratified the ERA within the first year. Indiana became the 35th, and last, state to ratify it in 1977. However, the next year Congress buckled and extended the ratification deadline to June 30, 1982. Nonetheless, conservative women were successful, and the ERA failed to be ratified by the necessary three-fourths of the states. In addition, five of the 35 states passed rescissions, changing their decisions about ratifying the ERA. Although ERA supporters claim these rescissions are invalid, the Constitution is silent about whether states may rescind ratifications.

The ERA was reintroduced in Congress on July 14, 1982, and has been before every session since then. It requires approval by two-thirds of both the House and Senate and ratification by 38 states. Sound impossible? ERA proponents are organized and determined.

Strategies for Ratification

They have two primary strategies to ratify the ERA:

- Starting from scratch. In recent sessions of the House, Rep. Carolyn Maloney (D-New York) has introduced legislation to include the ERA in the U.S. Constitution. The current bill in the 106th Congress is H.J. Res. 41; the Senate version is S.J. Res. 30. [As of April 2000, neither of those bills have been passed.]

- Going through the back door. A coalition effort is targeting specific states for ratification of the ERA originally passed in 1972. The ERA Summit has a "Three-State Strategy." This argues for validation of the 35 original ratifications and the verification of the ERA as part of the Constitution when three more states ratify it. The Summit does not recognize the five rescissions. It has targeted Illinois, Mississippi, Missouri, Oklahoma and Virginia for potential ratifications. Missouri reintroduced the ERA in its legislature on December 1, 1999.

The ERA Summit states on its Web site, "It is likely that Congress has the power to adjust or repeal the previous time limit on the ERA." Its advocate in the House is Rep. Robert Andrews (D-New Jersey). Along with nine cosponsors, Rep. Andrews introduced H. Res. 37 in the 106th Congress, which calls on the House to verify ratification of the ERA. [The bill has been referred to the House Subcommittee on the Constitution.]

Supporters cite the 27th Amendment, the Madison Amendment concerning congressional pay raises, as justification of their three-state strategy. Originally passed in 1789 *without a ratification deadline*, when there were only 13 states, it was ratified by a 38th state in 1992. However, not only did the ERA pass with a ratification deadline, it received a three-year extension *and still was unsuccessful*. The message was clear: America did not accept the ERA. And Congress tacked on an additional favor: To prevent more rescissions, it stipulated that only those states that had not ratified it could consider the ERA.

Columnist George Will correctly argues that the ERA would provide "license for judicial legislating, yielding what-

The ERA Would Exacerbate Society's Problems

The last thirty years have yielded mixed results for women as a group. Elites—those with the brains and money to attend college and pursue a career—have succeeded spectacularly. Others—those less talented, and often imprudent or unlucky in love (or sex)—are economically far worse off and far greater in number. Their misfortunes are depressingly familiar, the same things our antediluvian, pre-1960s mothers warned us against: unwanted pregnancies, single motherhood, poverty, and welfare dependency.

These problems are exacerbated by [the ERA,] a law that, in the name of equality, refuses to acknowledge sexual distinctions between men and women. The protections and special status the law once afforded mothers and wives because of their unique, biological sacrifices have been taken away; from a legal point of view they are now simply "spouses" judged on a par with men. We cannot estimate how many programs beneficial to women may have been curtailed or rejected (particularly in education) because of the cost or impracticality of providing the same for men. It works the other way around, too. Many states have cut back or eliminated successful all-male "boot camp" criminal rehabilitation programs because the states can't afford to run a parallel program for a relatively small number of female convicts. As a result, more young male offenders are released unrehabilitated—with predictably adverse effects on their future victims.

The interests of "women" are hardly advanced if they must live in a dysfunctional society. A society cannot function if it cannot make rules based on reason, experience, and the collective wisdom of its people.

Anita K. Blair, *Women's Quarterly*, Spring 1997.

ever meaning a result-oriented judge decided to discover in it." With the proliferation of activist judges in today's system, the ERA could easily be abused to serve the interests of radical feminists.

What the ERA Would Do for America

"In order to get the ERA back on track, people have to understand what they're missing," stated Eleanor Smeal, president of the Feminist Majority Foundation. While the federal ERA has not been ratified, some states have passed their own ERAs. In 1998, Florida and Iowa added ERA language to their constitutions. But what would the ERA do for America?

• Aid in the killing of millions of unborn babies. "Contraceptive coverage and reproductive freedom are the basic rights [of] women," writes Jennifer Baumgardner in *Jane*. "The ERA provides a legal base for actually attaining these bare-minimum rights." For example, state ERAs in New Mexico and Connecticut led to Medicaid coverage of abortions for poor women. The ERA would also eliminate waiting periods and spousal consent for abortion and mandate insurance coverage of contraception and abortions.

• Usher in homosexual rights. The ERA does not establish "equality" of the sexes, so much as it *eliminates differences* between them. With the ERA, lesbian women would be considered no different from men.

If the genders are the same, what difference is there in parenting situations? A New Jersey custody battle illustrates this. Two women—one a biological mother, the other a "psychological" parent—are fighting for custody of 5-year-old twins. "New Jersey's top court will have to deal with gay rights, the definition of marriage and the extent to which people who are not biologically related to a child can claim custody."

• Suppress true femininity and womanhood. The fight for "comparable worth"—or equal pay for similar work—resulted in shaming many women into the proverbial closet. Feminists fought to get all women into the labor force—never mind that not all wanted to join them. As a result, those who preferred part-time work, home-based business or stay-at-home motherhood were ridiculed.

One of these women has come out of the closet, bringing

her dust mop with her. "Today a repressive social code governs housekeeping, and those who breach it find themselves censured and shamed," writes author Cheryl Mendelson. "In the 1950s a woman vaunted her housekeeping and was sexually coy. Today you are supposed to display your sexuality and be coy about your housekeeping." Discussing the 1970s, Mendelson writes, "As women's on-the-job bona fides became accepted, the depreciation and social slighting of housewives . . . increased."

Mendelson affirms that not only have stay-at-home moms returned to domesticity, but intellectuals, teachers, struggling artists, and well-to-do doctors and lawyers have also rediscovered the joy of housekeeping. The women of Proverbs 31 are rising up.

Abolishing Differences Between the Sexes

"More than 27 years after Congress passed the ERA, nearly 23 years after the last state ratified it, more than 20 years after Congress's original ratification deadline passed, more than 17 years after the extended deadline passed," writes columnist George Will. "ERA supporters propose not just rewriting the rules of ratification but essentially abolishing all rules"—not to mention abolishing differences between the sexes. "Equality" has nothing to do with their struggle, but destroying our distinctions does.

Intrusive federal control is a major reason to oppose the ERA. "No matter how much legislation is in place, we are only one president or one Congress or one Supreme Court away from losing what we've gained," states Kim Gandy, executive vice president of the National Organization for Women. "We need a guarantee of equality as much now as we did then." ERA proponents are fighting for a change to the Constitution. This is nearly impossible to remove afterwards, regardless of what future generations want. Essentially, the "Second Wave" is scrambling to leave a permanent mark, its "last hurrah," before leaving the political arena.

Periodical Bibliography

The following articles have been selected to supplement the diverse views presented in this chapter. Addresses are provided for periodicals not indexed in the *Readers' Guide to Periodical Literature*, the *Alternative Press Index*, the *Social Sciences Index*, or the *Index to Legal Periodicals and Books*.

Marcia Ann Gillespie	"Get Out of the Kitchen," *Ms.*, May/June 1996.
Mary Ann Glendon	"A '70s Feminist Agenda Is an Insult to Women of the '90s," *Los Angeles Times*, September 5, 1995.
Wendy Kaminer	"A Civic Duty to Annoy," *Atlantic Monthly*, September 1997.
Audre Lorde	"Our Difference Is Our Strength," *Ms.*, July/August 1996.
Walter A. McDougall	"Sex, Lies, and Infantry," *St. Croix Review*, February 1998. Available from 3000 Zeeb Rd., Ann Arbor, MI 48106.
Wendy McElroy	"Whores vs. Feminists," *Liberty*, January 1999. Available from 1018 Water St., Suite 201, Port Townsend, WA 98368.
Elmira Nazombe	"Women's Rights as Human Rights: Imagine a World . . . ," *Christian Social Action*, December 1998. Available from 100 Maryland Ave. NE, Washington, DC 20002.
Paul Craig Roberts	"Feminist Fog in Foggy Bottom," *Washington Times*, April 7, 1997.
Sally L. Satel	"It's Always His Fault," *Women's Quarterly*, Summer 1997. Available from 2111 Wilson Blvd., Suite 550, Arlington, VA 22201-3057.
Cathy Young	"Out with the Old, in with the New," *Salon*, January 26, 2000. Available at www.salon.com/mwt/feature/2000/01/26/feminism/print.html.

For Further Discussion

Chapter 1

1. What evidence does Andrea C. Poe provide to support her claim that women are the victims of sexism? What evidence does Christina Hoff Sommers offer to support the opposite view? Whose argument is more convincing, and why?
2. Ida L. Castro and Elizabeth Fox-Genovese both utilize statistics to support their arguments about women's equality within the workplace. List the statistics provided by each of these authors. Do they contradict each other? Whose use of statistics is more persuasive? Explain your answer.
3. Germaine Greer argues that societal standards of beauty harm women. Karen Lehrman, in contrast, maintains that these standards can actually help women. Explain the arguments offered by these authors. Which do you agree with more, and why? What is your response to Lehrman's claim that society will always have standards of beauty for women?
4. Based on what you have read in this chapter, do you think American women are doing relatively well or relatively poorly? Give specific examples to support your claim.

Chapter 2

1. Both Elinor Burkett and Danielle Crittenden agree that feminism has expanded women's career opportunities. However, Crittenden argues that feminism has also limited women's personal choices by teaching women to forgo or postpone marriage and children. Do you agree or disagree with Crittenden's argument? Why or why not?
2. As explained by F. Carolyn Graglia, what are the consequences of the sexual revolution?
3. How do Leslie Anne Carbone and Phyllis Chesler differ in their definition of family? Which definition do you agree more with? Explain your answer.

Chapter 3

1. What evidence does Ginia Bellafante use to support her claim that feminism is no longer a serious political movement? How do Marcia Ann Gillespie and Carolyn Waldron refute Bellafante's claim? Whose argument is more convincing? Explain your answer.
2. Is the rhetorical device used by Charles Krauthammer—describing a major feminist tenet and explaining how feminists

have abandoned that tenet—effective in persuading you that contemporary feminists have betrayed their former principles? Why or why not? How would Susan Faludi respond to each of the assertions made by Krauthammer?

3. What assertions and assumptions do each of the authors in this chapter make about feminism? Which of these do you agree with, and why?

Chapter 4

1. According to Anne Roiphe, why must feminists support abortion rights? How does Maureen Jones-Ryan refute this claim? Whose argument is more persuasive? Why?

2. List the effects of pornography on women and society, as stated by Diana Russell and Wendy McElroy. Which of these effects do you agree with? Explain your answer.

3. Jennie Ruby and Karla Mantilla contend that feminists must join together to establish a set of global standards for women's rights. Paul Craig Roberts, on the other hand, maintains that for Western feminists to devise a set of global standards would be a form of "cultural imperialism"—the imposition of Western values on non-Western nations. Whose argument is more convincing? Explain.

4. Based on what you have read in the viewpoints by Patricia Ireland and the Concerned Women for America, do you believe that an equal rights amendment is necessary to uphold equal rights for women? Support your answer with specific reasons.

Organizations to Contact

The editors have compiled the following list of organizations concerned with the issues debated in this book. The descriptions are derived from materials provided by the organizations. All have publications or information available for interested readers. The list was compiled on the date of publication of the present volume; the information provided here may change. Be aware that many organizations take several weeks or longer to respond to inquiries, so allow as much time as possible.

American Civil Liberties Union (ACLU)
125 Broad St., New York, NY 10004-2400
(212) 549-2500 • publications ordering: 1-800-775-ACLU (2258)
e-mail: aclu@aclu.org • website: www.aclu.org
The ACLU champions the human rights set forth in the U.S. Constitution. It works to protect the rights of all Americans and to promote equality for women, minorities, and the poor. The organization publishes a variety of handbooks, pamphlets, reports, and newsletters, including the quarterly *Civil Liberties* and the monthly *Civil Liberties Alert*.

Association of Libertarian Feminists (ALF)
PO Box 20252, London Terrace PO, New York, NY 10011
website: www.alf.org
The purpose of ALF is to encourage women to become economically self-sufficient and psychologically independent; publicize and promote realistic attitudes toward female competence, achievement, and potential; oppose the abridgement of individual rights by any government on account of sex; work toward changing sexist attitudes and behavior exhibited by individuals; and provide a libertarian alternative to those aspects of the women's movement that tend to discourage independence and individuality. ALF publishes the quarterly newsletter *ALF News*.

Catalyst
120 Wall St., New York, NY 10005
(212) 514-7600 • fax: (212) 514-8470
e-mail: info@catalystwomen.org • website: www.catalystwomen.org
Catalyst is a national research and advisory organization that helps corporations foster the careers and leadership capabilities of women. Its information center provides statistics, print media, and research materials on women in business. It publishes a wide variety of reference materials, pamphlets, career guidance books,

and research reports, including *Advancing Women in Business: The Catalyst Guide to Best Practices from the Corporate Leaders.* It also publishes a career series for women searching for their first jobs and a monthly newsletter, *Perspective.*

Center for the American Woman and Politics (CAWP)
Eagleton Institute of Politics, Rutgers,
State University of New Jersey
191 Ryders Ln., New Brunswick, NJ 08901-8557
(732) 932-9384
e-mail: liphilli@rci.rutgers.edu
website: www.rci.rutgers.edu/~cawp/

CAWP is a research and public service organization for women in politics and government that encourages women's involvement in public life. It disseminates information about the backgrounds, status, and impact of women legislators; holds conferences and seminars about women in American politics; underwrites grants for specific, related projects; and takes surveys on women's issues. In addition to its newsletter *CAWP News and Notes*, the organization publishes books, monographs, and reports, including *Women as Candidates in American Politics, In the Running: The New Woman Candidate, Women Make a Difference,* and *Women's Routes to Elective Office: A Comparison with Men's.*

Center for Women Policy Studies (CWPS)
1211 Connecticut Ave. NW, Suite 312, Washington, DC 20036
(202) 872-1770 • fax: (202) 296-8962
e-mail: cwpsx@aol.com • website: www.centerwomenpolicy.org

CWPS is an independent feminist policy research and advocacy institution established in 1972. The center's programs combine advocacy, research, policy development, and public education to advance the agenda for women's equality and empowerment. CWPS programs address educational equity, family and workplace equality, violence against women, girls and violence, women's health, reproductive rights, and women and AIDS. The center publishes reports, articles, papers, bibliographies, and books such as *The SAT Gender Gap, Violence Against Women as a Bias-Motivated Hate Crime,* and *Guide to Resources on Women and AIDS.*

Eagle Forum
PO Box 618, Alton, IL 62002
(618) 462-5415 • fax: (618) 462-8909
e-mail: eagle@eagleforum.org • website: www.eagleforum.org

The Eagle Forum is dedicated to preserving traditional family values. It believes mothers should stay at home with their children, and it favors policies that support the traditional family and reduce government intervention in family issues. The forum opposes feminism, believing the movement has harmed women and families. The organization publishes the monthlies *Phyllis Schlafly Report* and *Education Reporter.*

Equality Now

PO Box 20646, Columbus Circle Station, New York, NY 10023
e-mail: info@equalitynow.org • website: www.equalitynow.org

Equality Now is an international human rights organization dedicated to action for the civil, political, economic, and social rights of girls and women. Taking advantage of both traditional and "high-tech" action techniques such as letter-writing and fax campaigns, video witnessing, media events, and public information activities, Equality Now mobilizes action on behalf of individual women whose rights are being violated and promotes women's rights at local, national, and international levels. The organization publishes the quarterly update *Words and Deeds.*

Family Research Council

801 G St. NW, Washington, DC 20001
(202) 393-2100 • fax: (202) 393-2134
e-mail: corrdept@frc.org • website: www.frc.org

The council is a conservative social policy research, lobbying, and educational organization. It promotes the traditional two-parent family in which the husband is the breadwinner and the wife stays home with the children. The council supports government policies that protect and promote the traditional family. It publishes the monthly newsletter *Washington Watch*, the bimonthly *Family Policy*, and reports such as *The American Family Under Siege.*

The Feminist Majority Foundation

1600 Wilson Blvd., Suite 801, Arlington, VA 22209
(703) 522-2214 • fax: (703) 522-2219
e-mail: femmaj@feminist.org • website: www.feminist.org

The Feminist Majority Foundation views feminism as a global movement dedicated to equality and seeks to eliminate discrimination of all kinds—sex, race, sexual orientation, age, religion, national origin, disability, and marital status. And, like feminists since the late nineteenth century, it advocates nonviolence and works to eliminate social and economic injustice. The foundation publishes the quarterly *Feminist Majority Report*, the Empowering

Women series of reports, as well as surveys on abortion clinic violence and a guide to teaching women's history.

Feminists for Free Expression (FFE)
2525 Times Square Station New York, NY 10108
(212) 702-6292 • fax: (212) 702-6277
e-mail: ffe@aol.com
website: www.pleiades-net.com/org/FFE.1.html
FFE, a not-for-profit organization, was founded in January 1992 in response to the many efforts to solve society's problems by book, movie, or music banning. FFE believes such efforts divert attention from the substantive causes of social ills and offer a cosmetic, dangerous "quick fix." FFE believes freedom of expression is especially important for women's rights. While messages reflecting sexism pervade our culture in many forms, sexual and nonsexual, suppression of such material will neither reduce harm to women nor further women's goals. FFE provides a leading voice opposing state and national legislation that threatens free speech; defends the right to free expression in court cases, including those before the Supreme Court; supports the rights of artists whose works have been suppressed or censored; and provides expert speakers to universities, law schools, and the media throughout the country.

Feminists for Life of America
733 15th St. NW, Suite 1100, Washington, DC 20005
(202) 737-FFLA
e-mail: comackay@erols.com • website: www.feministsforlife.org
Established in 1972, Feminists for Life is a nonsectarian, grassroots organization that seeks true equality for all human beings, particularly women. It opposes all forms of violence, including abortion, euthanasia, and capital punishment, as they are inconsistent with the core feminist principles of justice, nonviolence, and nondiscrimination. Its efforts focus on education, outreach, and advocacy, as well as facilitating practical resources and support for women in need.

Foundation/Feminists for a Compassionate Society
PO Box 868, Kyle, TX 78640-0868
(512) 447-6222
e-mail: ffacs@igc.apc.org • website: www.compassionate.org
The Foundation/Feminists for a Compassionate Society is a women-led feminist organization working to create social change based on the assumption that the capitalist, masculinist, and ego-

centric social and economic paradigm we currently function within must be replaced by a more giving, nonmilitaristic, and other-centered way of living. The foundation supports a variety of women-led projects such as the Feminist International Radio Endeavor (FIRE), the Women's International News Gathering Service (WINGS), and arts and activism.

The Heritage Foundation
214 Massachusetts Ave. NE, Washington DC 20002-4999
(202) 546-4400 • fax: (202) 546-8328
e-mail: info@heritage.org • website: www.heritage.org
The Heritage Foundation is a public policy research institute that advocates limited government and the free market system. It opposes affirmative action for women and minorities and believes the private sector, not government, should be relied upon to ease social problems and improve the status of women. The foundation publishes the bimonthly journal *Policy Review* as well as hundreds of monographs, books, and papers on public policy issues.

Male Liberation Foundation (MLF)
701 NE 67th St., Miami, FL 33138
(305) 756-6249 • fax: (305) 756-7962
MLF is a men's organization dedicated to counteracting feminist influence. It attempts to stop the rising divorce rate, to inform men that women now hold more power and money than men do, to motivate young men to achieve the career success that young women have, and to encourage women to be housewives. MLF believes men and women have distinct biological and psychological differences. It believes feminism has harmed men and male/female relationships and opposes all affirmative action legislation. The foundation publishes the monthly newsletter *Male Liberation Foundation* and a book titled *The First Book on Male Liberation and Sex Equality*.

National Coalition Against Censorship
275 Seventh Ave., New York, NY 10001
(212) 807-6222 • fax: (212) 807-6245
e-mail: ncac@ncac.org • website: www.ncac.org
The coalition comprises more than forty national nonprofit organizations united to preserve and advance freedom of thought, inquiry, and expression. It opposes censorship, including censorship of pornography, as "a dangerous opening to religious, political, artistic, and intellectual repression." The coalition educates the

public concerning the dangers of censorship. Its publications include the quarterly newsletter *Censorship News,* and reports.

National Coalition of Free Men (NCFM)
PO Box 129, Manhasset, NY 11030
(516) 482-6378
e-mail: ncfm@ncfm.org • website: www.ncfm.org
The NCFM is a nonprofit educational organization that examines the way sex discrimination affects men. It also tries to raise public consciousness about little known but important topics dealing with the male experience. NCFM sponsors a variety of projects and publishes the bimonthly *Transitions: Journal of Men's Perspectives* and the *NCFM Ezine Gazette* online newsletter.

National Council for Research on Women (NCRW)
11 Hanover Square, New York, NY 10005
(212) 785-7335 • fax: (212) 785-7350
e-mail: ncrw@ncrw.org • website: www.ncrw.org
NCRW, founded in 1981, is a working alliance of 84 women's research and policy centers, more than 3,000 affiliates, and a network of over 200 international centers. NCRW's mission is to enhance the connections among research, policy analysis, advocacy, and innovative programming on behalf of women and girls. It conducts research and education programs and acts as a clearinghouse. The council publishes an annual report, directories, and reports such as the *Girls Report* and *IQ: Women and Girls in Science, Math, and Engineering.* Its quarterly newsletter is titled *Women's Research Network News.*

National Organization for Women (NOW)
733 15th St. NW, 2nd Floor, Washington, DC 20005
(202) 628-8NOW (8669) • fax: (202) 785-8576
e-mail: now@now.org • website: www.now.org/
NOW is one of the largest and most influential feminist organizations in the United States. It seeks to end prejudice and discrimination against women in all areas of life. NOW lobbies legislatures to make laws more equitable and works to educate and inform the public on women's issues. It publishes the *National NOW Times,* policy statements, and articles.

NOW Legal Defense and Education Fund (NOW LDEF)
395 Hudson St., New York, NY 10014
(212) 925-6635 • fax: (212) 226-1066
email: ademarco@nowldef.org • website: www.nowldef.org

NOW LDEF pursues equality for women and girls in the workplace, the schools, the family, and the courts, through litigation, education, and public information programs. NOW LDEF also provides technical assistance to Congress and state legislatures, employs sophisticated media strategies, and organizes national grassroots coalitions to promote and sustain broad-based advocacy for women's equality. Established in 1970 by the founders of the National Organization for Women, NOW LDEF is a separate organization with its own mission, programs, and Board of Directors. The fund publishes books on topics such as reproductive rights and violence against women, legal resource kits, up-to-the-minute fact sheets, and surveys.

Third Wave Foundation
116 East 16th St., 7th Floor, New York, NY 10003
(212) 388-1898 • fax: (212) 982-3321
e-mail: ThirdWaveF@aol.com
website: www.feminist.com/3wave.htm

Third Wave is a national organization created by and for young women with the goal of building a lasting foundation for young women's activism around the country. As a grantmaking organization, its grantmaking efforts go toward reproductive rights, microenterprise, scholarships, and general organizing grants to young women's organizations across the country. Third Wave is led by a board of activist young women and men that reflects America's diversity, and it strives to combat inequalities that result from age, gender, race, sexual orientation, economic status, and level of education. The organization publishes the newsletter *See it? Tell it. Change it!*

Women Against Pornography (WAP)
PO Box 845, Times Square Station, New York, NY 10036
(212) 307-5055

WAP is a feminist organization that seeks to change public opinion about pornography so that Americans no longer view it as socially acceptable or sexually liberating. WAP offers slide shows, lectures, and a referral service to victims of sexual abuse and sexual exploitation. Its publications include *Women Against Pornography—Newsreport.*

Bibliography of Books

Elinor Burkett

The Right Women: A Journey Through the Heart of Conservative America. New York: Scribner, 1998.

Phyllis Chesler

Letters to a Young Feminist. New York: Four Walls Eight Windows, 1997.

Danielle Crittenden

What Our Mothers Didn't Tell Us: Why Happiness Eludes the Modern Woman. New York: Simon & Schuster, 1999.

Mary Daly

Quintessence—Realizing the Archaic Future: A Radical Elemental Feminist Manifesto. Boston: Beacon, 1998.

Geoff Dench

Transforming Men: Changing Patterns of Dependency and Dominance in Gender Relations. New Brunswick, NJ: Transaction, 1996.

Rene Denfeld

The New Victorians: A Young Woman's Challenge to the Old Feminist Order. New York: Warner Books, 1995.

Tom Digby, ed.

Men Doing Feminism. New York: Routledge, 1998.

Andrea Dworkin

Woman Hating. New York: Dutton, 1974.

Alice Echols

Daring to Be Bad: Radical Feminism in America, 1967–1975. Minneapolis: University of Minnesota Press, 1989.

Susan Faludi

Backlash: The Undeclared War Against American Women. New York: Crown, 1991.

Elizabeth Fox-Genovese

Feminism Is Not the Story of My Life: *How Today's Feminist Elite Has Lost Touch with the Real Concerns of Women.* New York: Anchor Books, 1996.

Betty Friedan

The Feminine Mystique. New York: W.W. Norton, 1963.

F. Carolyn Graglia

Domestic Tranquility: A Brief Against Feminism. Dallas: Spence, 1998.

Germaine Greer

The Whole Woman. New York: Knopf, 1999.

Sharon Hays

The Cultural Contradictions of Motherhood. New Haven, CT: Yale University Press, 1996.

Leslie Heywood and Jennifer Drake, eds.

Third Wave Agenda: Being Feminist, Doing Feminism. Minneapolis: University of Minnesota Press, 1997.

Patricia Ireland

What Women Want. New York: Dutton, 1996.

Christopher Lasch	*Women and the Common Life: Love, Marriage, and Feminism*. New York: W.W. Norton, 1997.
Karen Lehrman	*The Lipstick Proviso: Women, Sex & Power in the Real World*. New York: Doubleday, 1997.
Catharine A. MacKinnon	*Toward a Feminist Theory of the State*. Cambridge, MA: Harvard University Press, 1989.
Catharine A. MacKinnon and Andrea Dworkin, eds.	*In Harm's Way: The Pornography Civil Rights Hearings*. Cambridge, MA: Harvard University Press, 1997.
Nan Bauer Maglin and Donna Perry, eds.	*"Bad Girls"/"Good Girls": Women, Sex and Power in the Nineties*. New Brunswick, NJ: Rutgers University Press, 1996.
Anne Richardson Roiphe	*Fruitful: A Real Mother in the Modern World*. Boston: Houghton Mifflin, 1996.
Katie Roiphe	*The Morning After: Sex, Fear and Feminism on Campus*. Boston: Little, Brown, 1993.
Miriam Schneir, ed.	*Feminism in Our Time: The Essential Writings, World War II to the Present*. New York: Vintage Books, 1994.
Gloria Steinem	*Moving Beyond Words*. New York: Simon & Schuster, 1994.
Sheila Tobias	*Faces of Feminism: An Activist's Reflections on the Women's Movement*. Boulder, CO: Westview Press, 1997.
Rebecca Walker, ed.	*To Be Real: Telling the Truth and Changing the Face of Feminism*. New York: Anchor Books, 1995.
Naomi Wolf	*Promiscuities: The Secret Struggle for Womanhood*. New York: Random House, 1997.

Index